TINY TERROR

TINY TERROR

Why Truman Capote (Almost) Wrote
Answered Prayers

William Todd Schultz

OXFORD
UNIVERSITY PRESS

Oxford University Press, Inc., publishes works that further
Oxford University's objective of excellence in research,
scholarship, and education.

Oxford   New York
Auckland   Cape Town   Dar es Salaam   Hong Kong   Karachi
Kuala Lumpur   Madrid   Melbourne   Mexico City   Nairobi
New Delhi   Shanghai   Taipei   Toronto

With offices in
Argentina   Austria   Brazil   Chile   Czech Republic   France   Greece
Guatemala   Hungary   Italy   Japan   Poland   Portugal   Singapore
South Korea   Switzerland   Thailand   Turkey   Ukraine   Vietnam

Published by Oxford University Press, Inc.
198 Madison Avenue, New York, New York 10016

www.oup.com

Oxford is a registered trademark of Oxford University Press, Inc.

Library of Congress Cataloging-in-Publication Data

Schultz, William Todd.
   Tiny terror : why Truman Capote (almost) wrote Answered prayers / William Todd Schultz.
      p. cm. — (Inner lives series)
   Includes bibliographical references and index.
   ISBN 978-0-19-975204-1 (alk. paper)
   1. Capote, Truman, 1924-1984—Psychology. 2. Authors, American—20th century—
Biography. 3. Psychoanalysis and literature—United States. 4. Capote, Truman, 1924-1984
Answered prayers. I. Title.
   PS3505.A59Z875 2011
   813'.54—dc22
[B]   2010037233

9 8 7 6 5 4 3 2 1
Printed in the United States of America
on acid-free paper

To my mother and father

PREFACE

Truman Capote was my very first psychobiographical subject, back in 1986 at the University of California–Davis, where I studied at the time for my Ph.D. I'm still, after all these years, not sure why. I think the choice had mainly to do with my father, Richard Schultz. I recall his reading excerpts from the scandalous *Answered Prayers* as they appeared in *Esquire*. At some point in my library crawlings, I came across Capote on the magazine's cover, in black borsalino and black coat, sharpening his nails with a stiletto. Damage was getting done, the picture seemed to say, and Capote looked perfectly merciless. Who was this pint-sized puncturer?

I had read *In Cold Blood*, then *Breakfast at Tiffany's* and *Other Voices, Other Rooms* (which begins just as *In Cold Blood* does, with a "traveler" making his lonely way to a dust-choked, dead-end town). I recall my dad saying that, sentence for sentence, Capote had no peer (my brother disagreed). Anyway, the writing stirred me up first—the art—and psychological questions followed. But I had no clue how to proceed. I had never heard the word "psychobiography." Then I took a class from Alan Elms, a graduate seminar, and my eyes blinked wide in wonder. Here was the field I had been looking for; at long last a way to blend two powerful interests, fiction and psychoanalysis. I was hooked, and stayed hooked.

The paper I came up with was lousy, I see now. My question was worthy—why did Capote write *Answered Prayers*, why destroy the rich and famous "swans" he so adored?—but my answers, while generally in the ballpark, epitomized all those psychobiographical strategies I later came to detest. Green and casting about for a theory with which to assay Capote's complex interior, I stumbled onto, of all people, Wilhelm Reich. A colleague, David Philhour, was a Reich aficionado. He recommended *The Function of the Orgasm*, which I dutifully read and found amusing. Then I turned to the better *Character Analysis*, written before Reich broke with the Freudian model. Its idea was that personality amounted to character armor, a carapace layered over sensitive weak spots. Various types were elucidated, including what Reich called the "phallic-narcissist." Now, in hindsight, I can't off the top of my head recall what, exactly, this type amounted to, but I saw it then as fitting Capote nicely. So I made phallic-narcissism the core of my analysis. I fitted Capote for a diagnostic straitjacket. And that was that.

I don't remember what Alan Elms said about the essay. I know what I would say about it now if it had been written by one of my own students. Too much pathologizing. Too reductionist; overly simplistic. And especially: why Reich?

So I don't say my first effort was a success. But in crafting the argument—and before that, simply gathering the data—I fell in love with the process. It was archival; excitingly investigative; creative. The pursuit of the smoking gun hooked me. It still does. There is something a little mesmerizing about locating mysteries in people's lives, then fleshing these mysteries out and, finally, shedding what intensity of light one can on them. Capote made me a psychobiographer. And I repay a debt, of sorts, in writing this book.

One final pleasant aside: I had a friend who knew Dominick Dunne, who knew Capote. I told my friend's parents about my work. They sent it to Dunne, whom, of course, I never expected to hear from. But one month later, during a period of my life that might be charitably characterized as aimless, Dunne called me out of the blue. I was floored. He said he liked the piece; he also said he felt I got Capote exactly right (an overly kind suggestion, I think, but encouraging all the same). That fortified me a little. And I never forgot Dunne's generosity in reaching out to a young, infinitely callow stranger. If I had any doubts about my calling, they were now arrested. I forged ahead, and finished a doctoral dissertation centering on the life and creative work of James Agee, my second psychobiographical subject.

The title of this book's penultimate chapter comes from Norman Mailer. He's the one who described *Answered Prayers* as "frying the fancier fish." And just as it did in 1986, the question still intrigues me. Why, indeed, did Capote do it? Why plan a book that aimed to eviscerate a jet set in whose splendid company Capote had long loitered? Why tattle on trillionaires? Way back when, I glimpsed a few possible reasons; since then others have been added to the list.

What follows is the result of a roughly 25-year sojourn. I can't pretend to possess all the answers—that's far too much to ask of psychobiography. But I can recommend a few of the better vistas, a way of seeing what Capote was up to, whether he knew it himself or not. Capote always hoped *Answered Prayers* would represent a pinnacle of his creative powers. It never amounted to that. Yet it is, in so many different ways, the key to his life. My aim here is to show precisely how.

ACKNOWLEDGEMENTS

I want to thank Pacific University for the award of sabbatical leave in the spring of 2010. That leave made this book feasible. Lori Handelman, my editor at Oxford, was terrifically supportive, responsive, and astute. I cannot thank her enough. She is the editor everybody dreams of but rarely meets in reality. I had two magnificent research assistants who helped out a great deal: Danielle De Boer and Ashley Wang. My agent, Betsy Lerner, is a miracle. I wonder daily at my good fortune in simply meeting her, let alone calling myself one of her clients. She's a truly extraordinary, wise advocate. Finally, there could be no book without my three supreme and loving inspirations: Theresa Love, Adrienne, and Henry.

CONTENTS

INTRODUCTION: A SHORT PSYCHOBIOGRAPHY PRIMER

This book, like all the others in Oxford's *Inner Lives* Series, is a psychobiography. Some find that word hard to get their heads around. Others see it and feel a sudden spike in blood pressure. I want, therefore, to say a few words on the subject in order to (1) increase the circumference of noggins, and (2) prevent strokes.

Psychobiography is not biography. It is quite a bit more focused, selective. Biography is an exhaustively descriptive life-study, a massive, decades-long undertaking. It's all about the what, where, when, how, and who of the subject's life. Psychobiography zeros in on the *why*. Biographers talk about the *why*, too, but it's not their chief focus. The *why* is touched on, but typically undernourished. Psychobiographers flesh out the *why*, and they do so in a fashion they are uniquely suited for: by thoughtfully and judiciously applying psychological theory and experimental research. They use theory and research to shed light on subtext, to get at motives secreting themselves behind the life and, in this case, the art.

Biographers do not leave many stones unturned (sometimes to tedious effect). Psychobiographers do, on purpose. They selectively set their sights on some facets of the life above others. What I am most interested in here is Truman Capote's last, unfinished novel, *Answered Prayers*, in which he bit down hard on the smooth, socialite hands that fed him. To get there, I examine his childhood, some early novels, some short stories, and his murder masterpiece, *In Cold Blood*, but I also leave several books and stories unexamined.

I don't unpack *The Muses Are Heard* or *The Grass Harp*, for instance. I also gloss over certain relationships, while homing in on others more formative. For deliberately thorough accounts of Capote's life, Gerald Clarke's superb, insightful, fluidly written biography is a must-read; so is George Plimpton's endlessly entertaining oral history. The Capote letters, *Too Brief a Treat*, edited by Clarke, are another excellent resource, as are the many interviews Capote gave over the years, especially Lawrence Grobel's *Conversations with Capote* and M. Thomas Inge's *Truman Capote Conversations*. The point is, this book in your hands, while a decent life-survey, is necessarily incomplete. It's about, mainly, *Answered Prayers*. Clarke and Plimpton are far better sources if what you want is a long view of the life as a whole. On the other hand, if a pointedly *psychological* take on the life is what you are after, this book fits the bill. It's all about why Capote did what he did. It's about the *subjective origins* of his art, how his personality predetermined creative themes and needs in his work.

The word *personality* is important. I am attempting a personality profile. And personality is anything but slight. It includes traits (what some call "basic endogenous tendencies"), characteristic adaptations developed in response to traits, needs and motives, mechanisms of defense, common moods, attitudes, stories we tell ourselves and others about our life, single scenes containing affect and characters—the list is long. A lot of people seem to believe that what psychobiographers are after, more than anything else, is a diagnosis; a name one pins on stationary, one-dimensional targets. Not true. In fact, the odds are *good* that any psychobiography-by-diagnosis is *bad*. Think about it: Diagnoses are names. They describe a state of being, not its origin. They remove dynamics from the equation, pressing the person into static pigeonholes. Personality moves; diagnoses stay put. Plus, labels are tautological. It works like this: Person X is a borderline personality. Why? Because she cuts herself and fears abandonment. Why does she cut herself and fear abandonment? Because she is a borderline personality. It can be a pointless dance. For reasons like these and others, I stay away from diagnoses. I don't pin a label on Truman Capote. I don't find labels useful at all, and more to the point, they don't make sense of Capote's art, this book's aim.

So no labels get tossed around here, nor do I make much explicit use of Freudian theory. I single Freud out because, just like people assume psychobiographers diagnose subjects, they also assume psychobiography makes frequent use of psychoanalysis, as if psychobiography and Freud were somehow intrinsically connected. They aren't. Unlike most mainstream personality psychologists, I have nothing against Freud. I have read Freud widely and carefully (also unlike most mainstream personality psychologists). I think he was a genius. I think much of what he said—about repression, disguise, motives, defenses, sexuality, and affect displacement—is broadly on target. But psychobiography is an eclectic enterprise. Limiting oneself to a single theoretical structure, especially if done *a priori*— before sifting through the details of the life—is severely limiting and possibly damaging.

In studying Capote, reading his works, and rummaging through his colorful life history, two things struck me most forcefully. One, the importance of his early relationships, and how those relationships gave rise to a style of emotion-regulation that persisted into adulthood. And two, the fact that, as a writer, Capote reveled in the telling of stories that colonized much of his experience and crystallized personality patterns and needs. These two observations led me to two theories: *attachment theory* (mainly contemporary research by Phillip Shaver and Mario Mikulincer) and Silvan Tomkins's *script theory*. These models, it seemed clear to me, fit the life best. And as the estimable Alan Elms once said, if the theory glove fits, wear it. I do just that here. No doubt, theory choice in psychobiography is a tricky, partly subjective decision, just like most things in life, and most things in psychology, for that matter. But it works best when the life is the guide. The life points the way. And from there, the proof is in the pudding. Does the theory shed light, does it open doors onto the subject's essential mysteries? That's the abiding question.

There are two particular assertions about psychobiography one meets with frequently. Here is the first: *You can't analyze a dead person.* It is true—most psychobiography focuses on subjects no longer living. There is no special reason for that. It isn't as if living subjects were out of bounds. A subject is a subject, dead or alive. In fact, the first book in this series concerns the very alive George W. Bush. But psychobiography requires biography, and biographies usually don't come until after the person is gone. Biography is normally a posthumous art, so psychobiography is, too. That said, the "dead person" critique is really about access. It assumes that direct contact with a live subject increases the psychobiography's validity, that the live subject can be a guide of sorts, steering psychobiographers down fruitful avenues of understanding. Perhaps in the best of instances this is true; but in fact, most live subjects don't have the slightest interest in opening themselves up to a psychobiographer. I doubt George W. Bush, for instance, would have agreed, if asked, to comment on McAdams's interpretations of his psychological life or the question of why he invaded Iraq. A possibility like that is simply too much to hope for. It happens every now and then, but it's exceedingly rare. Also, odd as it may sound, people do not have privileged access to their own motives. If I want to know why Person X did Thing Y, asking him directly seems perfectly reasonable. It seems like the surest path to follow. But Person X may not know. Or, Person X may think he knows when he doesn't. In some cases Person X even lies or misleads, especially when his motives are unsavory. The simple fact is that people are poor at identifying reasons for the things they do. Built-in biases of various sorts get in the way, some having to do with the way people think, some with emotional blind spots. So a live subject isn't the advantage one might imagine it is. The dead don't talk, it's true; the living do, but what they say isn't always particularly helpful.

What is one to do, anyway, when a living subject disagrees with a psychobiographical interpretation? It's an interesting question. Something like this happened to Alan Elms when he published a psychobiographical essay on the still-living B.F. Skinner. Skinner had what he called a "dark year," a time when he tried writing a novel in his parents' basement before discovering the radical behaviorist ideology that came to define him. No novel emerged. The effort was a failure. Skinner spent most days puttering about, getting little work done. Elms, using Erikson's psychosocial model, calls the dark year "an identity crisis." Skinner tried on the novelist persona, then discarded it in favor of a different possible self, the outspoken, iconoclastic social philosopher, the arch-behaviorist. Elms makes a strong case: Skinner did seem to be in crisis, and the crisis did seem to get solved by the adoption of a new philosophy, a new style of life. But Skinner saw things differently. To Skinner, Elms was off track, his conclusions invalid. So was Elms wrong? Does Skinner's opinion trump Elms's? No, it doesn't; at least not automatically. The living subject's reaction is always interesting; it is more data to take in, more thought to account for, but it isn't intrinsically superior to opinions of others. Skinner's wife, for instance, thought Elms was exactly right. Does that mean the wife was right and Skinner wrong? Maybe, maybe not.

I had a similar experience, though it ended differently. I wrote a short essay on the writer Kathryn Harrison. In it I argued that her adolescent visit to a gynecologist where she was fitted, at her mother's insistence, for a diaphragm, came to be especially self-defining. I called the visit Harrison's "prototypical scene." Somehow I got Harrison's address and sent her the paper, which she was happy to read and comment on. What ensued was a long discussion. She told me what she thought about what I said, and I told her more of what I thought. It was a valuable exchange. It gave me new ideas, fresh ways of thinking about her life and about the prototypical-scene concept, but my view of the gynecologist visit's importance stayed intact. We reached a happy accord, neither totally won over by the other's point of view. We agreed to disagree. And she was fine with that.

Here's the second assertion one runs into often: *Psychobiography is too reductionistically focused on childhood.* Whenever causes or reasons are adduced, there will be some reduction. It is unavoidable. Flooding in ecosystems causes numerous downstream effects. Earthquakes cause tsunamis; they also cause buildings to crumble and fall. Smoking causes heart disease, lung cancer, and strokes. All these formulations are reductionist; they trace effects to origins.

Psychobiography also traces effects to origins. Sometimes the origins concern the subject's childhood; sometimes, as in McAdams's book on Bush, they do not. Usually it is the case that decides things. Capote is on record saying "everything that's important happened to me then"—during childhood, that is. I agree. Psychobiographer and subject see eye to eye. Childhood can be decisive; it sets a tone and atmosphere; relationships form; strategies evolve and calcify, forming internalized models directing future action. When the childhood is key, psychobiographers need to show how and why. They make a case. And if the case works, if it achieves cogency, reductionism worries evaporate.

People always ask what kind of truth psychobiography achieves. What does it really mean to say a case works? What kind of truth does *anything* achieve? There are facts and there are interpretations. Psychobiography deals with both. It's a fact that Capote tried writing the book *Answered Prayers*; explaining why requires interpretation. Psychobiography succeeds when interpretations achieve inevitability. Facts converge on them naturally, softly. As a student of mine once said, they hatch. Interpretations *hatch*. Answers in psychobiography aren't true in some immortal, absolute sense. Truth is more *direction* than *destination*. We can be on track, but we never arrive; the trip doesn't end. So, setting Truth aside, I think it's best to say psychobiography either works or doesn't. Some people refer to this as "narrative truth," coherence as opposed to correspondence. My aim is to make Capote's life story "cohere"—to the degree anyone's really coheres.

Life is blurry; personality, too. We begin and end in mystery. The eyeball cannot see itself. So this book is a grainy image, a smudgy snapshot. But Capote is there. Not perfectly resolved, but there. A kind of lovely shadow.

TINY TERROR

1 | CONSISTENTLY INCONSISTENT CONSISTENCY

"Consistently inconsistent" is what Truman Capote liked to call himself. And maybe he was: we all are, actually. There is much less unity in personality than we like to believe—not *none*, but *less*.[1] But Capote was flagrantly consistent about at least one matter: when describing his early life, he always told the same two stories. It may be that neither is true, it may be that each is partly true; but it makes no difference. False memories tell us just as much about a person as true memories do, sometimes more.

Here's the first story:

It was a certain period of my life. I was only about two years old, but I was very aware of being locked in this hotel room. My mother was a very young girl. We were living in this hotel in New Orleans. She had no one to leave me with. She had no money and she had nothing to do with my father. She would leave me locked in this hotel room when she went out in the

---

1. Psychologists call this "domain specificity." Coping strategies that work in one setting may not work in others; goals that drive behavior during one period of life may fade during others. Different feelings, thoughts, and behaviors get elicited by different demands and situations.

evening with her beaux and I would become hysterical because I couldn't get out of this room. . . . I can't remember anything about that whole period except things like that. Because very soon after that I was separated from her.[2]

Elsewhere Capote was more attuned to the emotional devastation the episode entailed. He told Gerald Clarke, "Eventually I would become so exhausted that I would just throw myself on the bed or on the floor until they came back. Every day was a nightmare, because I was afraid they would leave me when it turned dark. I had an intense fear of being abandoned, and I remember practically all my childhood as being lived in a state of constant tension and fear."

Capote made frequent use of this particular scenario. It was the sort of story he dusted off with special devotion. The writer John Knowles, Capote's neighbor, and famous in his own right for the classic novel *A Separate Peace*, says:

Truman often talked about himself. Oh, my God, yes. . . . Just after I first met him, Truman began telling me his life story. This terrible, tragic story. The central tragedy (as he saw it) in his life is a scene: Truman is two years-old. He wakes up in an utterly strange room, empty. He yells, but he's locked in there. He's petrified, doesn't know where he is—which is in some dumpy hotel in the deep South—and his parents have gone out to get drunk and dance; they have locked this tiny little boy in this room. That was his image of terror, and I think it was his way of

---

symbolizing the insecurity of his youth—this image of that kind of abandonment.

There are a few things to notice about this memory right away. In the first version, it's his mother who was locking him in—and, according to Clarke, "instructing the staff not to let him out even if he screamed"—whereas in the other two it was his mother *and* father. So the facts varied slightly, as they often will when we recall early events from our lives. There's also the question of accuracy. Capote was just two years old. He said he was "very aware" of being locked in the room, but that's unlikely. More likely is the possibility that Capote reconstructed the scene from the vantage point of adulthood, maybe after being told about it by his mother, or someone else in the know. But the singularity of the scene—"I can't remember anything about that whole period except things like that"—its saliency, lends it special power. It colonized Capote's experience and drew other memories—or fantasies or dreams— into its orbit. Here, for instance, is a memory Capote called his "*very* earliest":

> I was probably three years old, perhaps a little younger, and I was on a visit to the St. Louis Zoo, accompanied by a large black woman my mother had hired to take me there. Suddenly there was pandemonium. Children, women, grown-up men were shouting and hurrying in every direction. Two lions had escaped from their cages. Two bloodthirsty beasts were on the prowl in the park. My nurse panicked. She simply turned and ran, leaving me alone on the path. That's all I remember about it.

Here again, it's hard to know, maybe impossible, if the scene really happened. But it doesn't matter, if it's *psychologically* true.

Clarke, for what it's worth, calls the zoo memory "undoubtedly a dream rather than an actual event," though he does see it as "symbolic of [Capote's] early years." The zoo memory and the memory of the hotel room read like two versions of the same basic experience. In both, Capote is around the same age. In both, his mother is implicated—she either rejects and abandons him or hires someone who flees when he's traumatized. Whatever the case, he is left alone to deal with overwhelming fear. For Capote, the hotel incident was nightmarish; with the zoo, the metaphor was "pandemonium." Either way, there was a loss of emotional control, the sense that the world was dangerous, that adults who ought to be available and responsive in the face of danger simply could not be counted on for comfort. They disappointed him terribly. They didn't come through. Capote was on his own to do what he could with the hand dealt him.

This last element is more of a stretch, but I do think it's especially striking: In *Other Voices, Other Rooms*, Capote's first novel, which he described as an "attempt to exorcise demons," he created a black female character he named, of all things, "Zoo." She owns a charm that keeps "anything terrible from happening." Capote's child alterego in the book, Joel Knox, tells Zoo, "I love you because you've got to love me because you've got to." But Zoo is crazy, "always talking about snow, always seeing things," and just like the black caretaker did in the zoo memory, Zoo (the character) leaves Joel just as he begins to place his trust in her. She runs to Washington, D.C., and though she promises to send for Joel once she gets established there, she never does.

What does it all mean? It means that Capote was haunted by a particular script. He's small and defenseless, in some strange and lonely place, and those whom he expresses love to, or those whom he relies on, people he justifiably trusts, leave him and let him down.

As Capote himself explained, "My underlying motivation was a quest for some sense of serenity, some particular kind of affection." But as a young boy, he had neither. In fact, "bloodthirsty beasts were on the prowl," feelings he could not control or escape.

This next memory is more lighthearted—practically farcical—but just as representative. Whereas the first two concern psychological conflicts in Capote's *life*, the third concerns his motives for *writing*. I want to describe several different versions as a way of highlighting how discrepant they are.

The following comes from a *Paris Review* interview with Pati Hill conducted in 1957. Hill asked Capote when he first started writing.

> When I was a child of about ten or eleven and lived near Mobile . . . I joined the Sunshine Club that was organized by the Mobile Press Register. There was a children's page with contests for writing. . . . The prize for the short-story writing contest was either a pony or a dog, I've forgotten which, but I wanted it badly. I had been noticing the activities of some neighbors who were up to no good, so I wrote a kind of *roman à clef* called "Old Mr. Busybody" and entered it in the contest. The first installment appeared one Sunday, under my real name. . . . Only somebody suddenly realized I was serving up a local scandal as fiction, and the second installment never appeared. Naturally, I didn't win a thing.

Here, now, is Capote to Lawrence Grobel; Grobel's interviews were conducted between 1982 and 1984, when Capote died.

> Mrs. Lee [the writer Harper Lee's mother] was quite an eccentric character. Mr. Lee was wonderful, but Mrs. Lee—who was

a brilliant woman—was an endless gossip. So I wrote something called "Mrs. Busybody" about Mrs. Lee and sent it to the *Mobile Register*. I won second prize and they printed the whole thing and it was just ghastly. . . . They were very upset in Alabama. . . . I didn't know it was going to be published! I just sent it in. . . . And then one Sunday, there it was. Then people started to whisper about me. . . . I found they were very upset about it. I was a little hesitant about showing anything after that. I remember I said, "Oh, I don't know why I did that, I've given up writing." But I was writing more fiercely than ever.

Once more the facts shift, or reverse themselves entirely. Was it Mr. or Mrs. Busybody? Who knows? Did the piece ever appear in print; did Capote win a prize; did the neighbors really whisper? It's anybody's guess. Eugene Walter, a writer and Mobile resident, had this to say:

His aunt realized that he had written about a next-door neighbor and called off publication. Truman had used an eccentric recluse for Mr. Busybody. . . . Truman pretended all his life that "Old Mr. Busybody" had been published. . . . That his first publication was on the Sunshine Page. . . . But it was never published. Nobody knows what happened to "Old Mr. Busybody," because his aunt grabbed it in a hurry. . . . There are people working on their doctorates, or whatever, searching the files of the *Mobile Press-Register* to this day.

There you have it. The story never saw the light of day. Capote made it all up—or most of it, at least. He wrote the piece, it seems, but it ruffled no feathers, thanks to his aunt.

What is enormously revealing about the tale as a whole, however, is the light it sheds on Capote's urge to write. The key detail is not the story's subject—Mr. or Mrs. Busybody—or the subject's inspiration. What is truly significant is the reaction Capote imagined. The work "upset people." The response was "ghastly." A scandal ensued. Neighbors talked. A little, modest *roman à clef* provoked major turmoil, but it strengthened Capote's resolve. He began to write more fiercely than ever. He said he had "given up," yet he did the opposite.

"Busybody" is a forerunner of Capote's situation with *Answered Prayers*, this book's chief focus. His very first story mirrors his last. *Answered Prayers* also was a *roman à clef*. It told the truth in fictional form. Temporarily it caused Capote to doubt his motives. Just like "Busybody," *Answered Prayers* essentially tattled, only on a grander scale. He scorched the rich and famous, printed details told to him in confidence by socialites and jet-setters who thought they were his friends, who thought he could be trusted, who never suspected he might betray them. And the reaction was the same: utter scandal. Erstwhile friends did more than whisper. They blacklisted him; shut him out of their lives forever.

Sometimes, when we engage in the act of remembering, we alter details in accordance with contemporary concerns; we inject a lot of the "present" into the "past." That is what Capote did here. "Busybody" became a foil for *Answered Prayers*. In talking about the former, Capote really signified the latter. He made the two experiences fit together. What confirms this is the fact that the connection was not lost on him. He said to Lawrence Grobel, "[Busybody] was sort of like when I began publishing those chapters of *Answered Prayers* and everybody was so upset." The element of timing is also relevant. Capote dated the beginning of *Answered Prayers* variously, but the two years he mentioned more than others were 1956 and

1958. The *Paris Review* interview in which he described "Busybody" appeared in 1957. So, when talking about the story, the book was very much on his mind. He saw "Busybody" through the prism of *Answered Prayers*.

Finally, even before any excerpts from *Answered Prayers* appeared in *Esquire*, Capote foresaw reactions similar to those he had imagined for "Busybody." He told *Rolling Stone* in 1973: "I'm sure [the book] will get some of the supreme all-time flat-out attacks." Then later, "[It will] kill my last chances in the world of ever winning anything. Except, perhaps, twenty years in jail."

The solution to the mystery of "Busybody," then, is that it was a junior substitute for *Answered Prayers*; it was *Answered Prayers* writ small. The present was projected into the past. And maybe most importantly of all, "Busybody"/*Answered Prayers* highlights one particular motive at the root of Capote's creativity: power. Here was a displaced boy thought to be excessively feminine, abandoned by his parents, raised by spinsterish aunts, always considered odd and eccentric, going exactly nowhere, fast. What might he do to make a way for himself? To find meaning? To get noticed? He would write. Words would become his weapons. With words, Capote made himself mighty. As he put it in one of his last remarks about the fallout from *Answered Prayers*, "I can't understand why everybody's so upset. What do they think they had around them, a court jester? They had a writer."

It is remarkable how two "memories," in their microcosmic fashion, can say so much about who a person is and why he did the things he did. In their basic architecture they embed a massive amount of life-history information. The first in particular I am inclined to nominate as a "prototypical scene," in a sense I will explain later. But for now, other matters warrant more immediate attention. It is essential, first, to investigate the facts of Capote's childhood, the events and happenings and relationships that resulted in the fixity of episodes like the "hotel room" and "Busybody." Those two memories colonized Capote's early experiences; next we need to explore exactly *how*.

2 | A SNAKE'S NEST OF NO'S

Until he simply got tired of the subject and all its mainly self-generated hype, Capote was emphatic when it came to his work-in-progress, *Answered Prayers*: "It is the only true thing I know. . . . I was born to write the book. . . . It means *everything*." About his childhood he was equally decisive: "*Everything* important really happened to me then." So, the book that meant everything emerged from a childhood when everything important happened. In fact, it's clear that in most important respects, the former was the logical outcome of the latter.

The signal twin facts of Capote's early life are these: his mother Lillie Mae, later called Nina, was a beautiful, doomed narcissist and fervid social-climber, a delicate flower straight out of Tennessee Williams. His father, Arch Persons, was a shiftless, feckless con man who never met a promise he minded breaking, least of all with respect to Truman. Neither was what Capote needed—an available, responsive parent. And it seems that he was not what they needed either—a child, in the way.

In almost every interview he ever gave, Capote laid out (not always terribly accurately) the basic outline of his "Southern gothic" origins. It was a Flannery O'Connor universe, minus the fervent religion.

Capote's father, Arch, was born and raised in Alabama, so "fast" in his ways that fellow Alabamans figured him for a Yankee. His orientation was manic—he walked fast, talked fast, and thought fast, according to Gerald Clarke, Capote's biographer. And he was no different with the ladies, most of whom found him all too beguiling, despite his thinning blond hair and thick eyeglasses.

Arch and Lillie married on August 23, 1923, on the brink of his twenty-sixth birthday. "It was a sad, sad day," said her brother Seabon. "She should have known better." Lillie was 16 at the time, and, according to Capote, "very, very beautiful—a Beauty Contest-winner type of child." "My mother was always running off to do something or other. She was what you might call a Southern Belle, always doing things, always interested in improving her mind. . . . Later on in life [she] became an enormously sensitive and intelligent person. But she was only sixteen when she married—a normal, beautiful girl, rather wild."

Though Arch had always believed it was his destiny to find massive wealth, the honeymoon by train to the Gulf coast got cut short due to lack of funds. That must have given Lillie pause. She had figured Arch, the "entrepreneur," as her magic ticket from nowhere to somewhere. In any case, whether she doubted him or not made scant difference when, in the winter of 1924, Lillie fainted during an exercise class and learned she was pregnant. As Clarke says, "It wasn't a happy discovery." Her plan was to abort—not an easy prospect in 1924, if ever. She made Arch aware of her intentions, "pleading, cajoling, and arguing with him all through the spring." But to no avail. Arch stalled, badly wanting a baby boy, despite the by-now-obvious fact that the marriage was in trouble. He sent Lillie away to a resort in Colorado where the climate was "wonderful." Her cousin, Jennie, brought her down to New Orleans when the time came near, and Truman Steckfus Persons was delivered at 3:00 P.M., September 30.

Arch had work with a steamship company, at which he excelled. They called him the line's "Prince Charming." But he never stopped scheming for something more, something outrageously lucrative. To him, money was the sixth sense, without which the other five were "of no avail." His own mother came to conclude that he simply didn't know right from wrong; the sheriff instinctively rattled his keys whenever Arch came to town. He wrote bad checks when funds got tight—for which he was tossed in jail. He also secretly arranged to have Lillie drive bootleg liquor around so he could make deliveries at night, his weak eyes not up to the job. Fed up and sick of the never-ending nonsense, Lillie resorted to affairs that Arch pathetically ignored. They'd trudge off to the movies, Arch always in the front row due to his poor eyesight, and Lillie would slip out to meet lovers, returning at the movie's end.

It was at this time that the hotel room incident occurred, with tiny Capote placed in a kind of lock-up while his parents pursued their sordid agendas. At last, after seven years of something loosely resembling marriage, Lillie informed Arch she was through. Returning to town after a stint in beauty school in New York, she took 15 minutes letting him know it was over. There was, moreover, another man. Habitually self-pitying, Arch called her greedy and unprincipled. No matter—the divorce was filed in August, 1931, though not actually finalized until November. Arch dodged the sheriff whose task it was to serve him the papers.

Arch used to call Truman his "little angel." But though the terms of the divorce initially allowed Arch three months' custody of the boy in a given year, the little angel rarely saw his father. Once Arch promised to buy lunch for Truman and friends, only to ask for the two dollars Truman brought along with him. It was one disappointment after another. Simply put, Capote never really had a father. Or, he *had* one, but Arch never paid him much mind, which is worse than not having one at all.

Capote's thoughts on these events are interesting. He was clear about the fact that he "very seldom" saw his father. But from there, things get trickier. As he put it, "My parents had more or less decided to live different lives. I never really cared if [Arch] would come or if he didn't come at all. . . . You know, the only way people can ever hurt me is if I let them get close to me. . . . I'm very careful about that, about who I get close to." Later in this chapter I explore attachment-based reactions in close detail; they are far and away the key ingredient of Capote's psychology, and central to the construction of his book *Answered Prayers*. But it's worth pausing now to notice Capote's responses to Arch's basic unavailability. One, he professed not to care. He suppressed and minimized feeling. He might have done the opposite; he might have upped the ante, raised the emotional temperature as a means of provoking a response. But he didn't. He chose an opposite avenue. Second, Capote introduced a strategy he would employ his entire life: Don't get close to anyone you figure may hurt you. Don't make yourself vulnerable. In fact, become as *invulnerable* as possible. Invulnerability was achieved by Capote in two ways: first, keep a close rein on your affections. And, as we saw in Chapter 1, attack threats when necessary, à la the Busybody affair. I see these responses as closely aligned; I want merely to note them for now.

Capote's father was a more important figure in his life than most people surmise. He affected Truman's fiction in a number of ways, especially early works like *Other Voices, Other Rooms*. But Lillie Mae, or Nina, is monumentally significant too; their relationship is quite a bit more complex.

Opinions about Lillie range far and wide. No one who knew her walked away unimpressed. Typically she's called "childlike," a case of arrested development, "amazed at everything," pursuing "adolescent values well into her thirties." Beautifully dressed, mannered, with "a great feeling for style," charming (though "you never felt she meant it," according to some), few found her anything but extremely beguiling, "very attractive sexually." She was a seductress. And she was jealous of competition. If her second husband, Joe Capote—a round little man just slightly taller than Nina, a Cuban with a promising future on Wall Street—snuck a sideways glance at women, Lillie promised to "get the carving knife."

Her life as it unrolled, abetted for a time by Joe's income, revolved around social climbing. Pursuit of high times trumped every prosaic demand of motherhood. As a Capote friend put it, "She scared me. Because she was not like a mother." Her ambition knew few bounds. "She wanted to be a member of café society, as it was called in those days, and she pursued it with determination. She entertained, spent money, lived well." Gerald Clarke compared her to a lovely plant stunted by lack of light. "She blossomed under the sunshine" of a prosperous marriage to Joe, transforming herself by dint of sheer force of personality "from an unsophisticated country girl into a woman of worldly tastes and glamorous occupations."

There would be two other pregnancies. But on those occasions Nina got her wish: she terminated both. "I will not have another child like Truman," she told Joe, by which she seemed to mean no other child could compare. "And if I do have another child"—a chance that never materialized, after one abortion left permanent damage—"it will be like Truman." An odd statement, to be sure. What she seems to be saying is that she both did and did not want another son like the one she already had, and mainly, at least obliquely, rejected.

Phoebe Vreeland, a writer and former magazine editor who met Capote at a party in Greenwich Village when Capote was twelve, had a close-up, regular view of Nina over the years. Her particular take on Lillie's identity provides a kind of summary opinion. "She was never someone with a terribly strong hold on life. She didn't know what she wanted. She was the kind of person you could have given anything, I mean anything—a big apartment—but who had no idea of what could please her."

For his part, Capote professed a protective love for his mother. Her parents had died when she was very young; she was adopted by three elderly ladies and an elderly uncle, raised in the same household as Truman, in effect living the same early life, a fact remarkable in its own right. She simply "wasn't able to cope," he said. And although he added, "I loved her very much," he also admitted "I never really saw her." In a different interview he made a nearly identical statement, this time about both parents, not just Nina: "I was loved by my mother and father, but I never saw them." Yet another perplexing reflection. The former—love—would seem to be contradicted by the latter—no contact. Again Capote dealt with the emotional meaning of unpleasant facts by suppression of feeling.

In reality, love was uncertain, and Capote was frequently devastated. As Clarke describes, "Truman was desolate when [Nina] drove off; once finding a perfume bottle she had forgotten, he drank it to the bottom, as if he could bring back the woman with her scent." There were occasions on which she'd promise to take him with her, away from eccentric aunts and small-town tedium to the glitter and rouge of big-city spectacle. "But after three days," he said, "she left. And I stood in the road, watching her drive away in a black Buick, which got smaller and smaller and smaller. Imagine a dog, watching and waiting and hoping to be taken away. That is the picture of me then."

Whenever Lillie did make contact, in torturously brief interludes, she tended to nag, bully, and belittle. Truman's effeminacy

embarrassed and irritated her. She used to wish, with bizarre obliviousness, or perhaps from a mindset of complete denial, that "Truman
would find a nice girl and settle down." She didn't always want a son;
but she claimed to pine for grandchildren.

Clarke's final estimate of Nina and her place in Capote's psychology is astute. "She did not hate him; if she had, he could at least have
hated her in return. . . . Nor, though she continued to dump him in
the laps of other people, did she really ignore him. . . . What she did
was worse. . . . She regarded him with ambivalence: she loved him
and she did not love him; she wanted him and she did not want
him; she was proud to be his mother and she was ashamed of him."
It would be hard for the most sinister psychologist to concoct a
more crazy-making formula. It's truly a wonder Capote never went
entirely insane. That he did not do so is a testament to his courage
and resiliency; even as a girlish boy, he was recognized by all around
him to be, whatever else he was or would one day become, tough as
nails. That quality, at least, rarely let him down.

Most of what Capote said about his early years is unsurprising
given the dismal biography. He called it "ghastly." He said he was
"very lonely." He had zero "sense of being particularly wanted by
anybody." In sum, "I never felt I belonged anywhere. . . . I had the
most insecure childhood I know of. . . . It was just total emotional
neglect. . . . I certainly don't feel as though I had any sturdy foundation to stand on. . . . When I was five, living in Alabama, I might as
well have been a deaf mute." And as far as Lillie Mae/Nina goes,
"She was the single worst person in my life."

A story from around this time, possibly another tall tale like those
in Chapter 1, provides some comic relief. Capote always insisted
he understood everything. "I was a very, very, super-intelligent child,
beyond anything you've ever seen," he boasted. One wouldn't know
this from his class work, however. Year after year, he failed the

simplest of subjects, "out of loathing and boredom." In biology, for instance, he spent all his time combing his hair. "Please put that comb away!" his teacher railed, to no effect. Tantrums were commonplace. He played hooky twice a week and was "always running away from home." He was thought somewhat eccentric and stupid, which he "suitably resented." In due course his principal called on his family, and told them that, in his opinion, and the opinion of most of the faculty, Capote was "subnormal." The sensible and humane action, it was felt, was to send him to some special program "equipped to handle backward brats." But at the eleventh hour, Capote proved objectively something he'd always privately recognized. One fateful day, the Works Progress Administration sent a team of researchers to town to administer intelligence tests to children. Capote's result? "I received the highest score they'd ever encountered." The next day the team returned and asked him to take the test again, apparently regarding the first result as something of a fluke. Again he scored "phenomenally high." Next, Capote, at the tester's request, traveled to New York accompanied by an aunt to tackle yet another test, this time at the Horace Mann School. "I came home a genius," he reported, "so proclaimed by science," with an IQ of 215, the "highest intelligence of any child in the United States."

All possible exaggeration aside, this was a signal moment. A young life defined depressingly as a "snake's nest of No's"—no parents to speak of, no friends but books, no hope, no future—finally met with one resounding "Yes." Now Capote knew at least one good thing for sure, vouchsafed by science. He was eccentric *because* he was a genius. His oddness was a *good* thing. "I always thought of myself as a kind of two-headed calf. . . . That was the first time I ever felt proud of myself and I flaunted the test results. . . . They now knew I wasn't retarded." As if the test outcome provided a license to do so, the necessary psychological ballast, Capote began feigning sickness just to stay home from school and read. In short order, writing became an obsession, something he felt he had no control over. In one room he made himself a little office with an old type-writer and worked for a number of hours every day; by his teens, he reckons, he had developed a definite style. "I began staying up all night, writing in a state of feverish excitement." A ninth-grade English teacher shared one of Truman's stories with a colleague, C. Bruner-Smith, without saying Capote had written it. In dream-like fashion, the work described the sensation of rolling down a hill and tumbling into unconsciousness. "It was a rather lengthy manu-script," Bruner-Smith recalls, "and I was struck and impressed by it. . . . It had a feeling I found very remarkable. . . . I couldn't believe that a boy of thirteen or fourteen could have produced it."

Many years later, Capote would observe, tellingly, "I've never been psychoanalyzed. That's all I want to say about it. I've never even consulted a psychiatrist. . . . *I work out all my problems in my work*." What's obvious is that writing saved Capote's life. Statements like that get made all the time, by and about all sorts of artists; on average, they tend towards hyperbole. Not so in this instance. By all accounts Capote was a very disturbed child. Writing—and intelligence—afforded Capote a gift around which he could craft a sense of self that affirmed his existence. There really was little else. Piles of undesired selves stacked up ominously for Capote to embody—runaway, hysteric, imbecile—but "writer" elbowed them decisively aside, and from the impossibly callow age of ten there was no looking back. Capote was a genius; he knew it and he proved it. And he discovered, by trial and error, like we all do in the beginning, that problems of whatever sort—and Capote's existed in wondrous variety—had a way of receding whenever he sat down in his little room at his typewriter and stepped into fantastical worlds of his own creation, under his complete power and control. This was a land of unreality superior to what he saw all around him. Writing was escape. It was also revenge—against the hand dealt him, against all who would do him wrong. This formula stayed intact. It goes a long way towards making sense of what Capote was up to with *Answered Prayers*.

The writing never stopped; nor did the problems it helped Capote surmount. In 1954, Nina Capote committed suicide. Truman was 29, in Europe when he got the news, making the film *Beat the Devil* with John Huston and Humphrey Bogart. Nina had overdosed before, but a friend had summoned help. This time, she washed down her Seconals with a hefty helping of alcohol; when Joe Capote found her the next morning, the phone was off the hook, indicating she'd tried calling someone. But the urge to die stifled whatever instinct for life remained.

Joe's accreting infidelities—a blow to her pride, to her sense of herself as a beautiful, stylish, attractive woman—had wounded her deeply; he'd also lost his job and most of their money with it. He'd been gambling in the volatile textile commodity market, siphoning money from his Wall Street employers. To escape jail, Joe had left for Cuba, with Nina in tow. They'd soon returned to New York, however, poorer than ever. So long as Nina had money, she was able to maintain her "society woman" pretense, the identity that meant the world to her. When the money disappeared, "that façade was shattered," according to Clarke. And Nina *was* the façade.

For years, Capote never talked about the way his mother died; outsiders were told she succumbed to pneumonia, insiders left mainly in the dark until many years later, when Capote at last came clean with the facts. Nina had been ashamed of Truman's homosexuality—wishing he were a "linebacker," not some gay genius—now it was his turn to be ashamed of her. On a superficial level, the death must have come as a relief. Nina was a constant problem.

"She was Jekyll and Hyde," Capote said, "much more neurotic and difficult than anybody realized." "There was something almost hysterical in her fluttering," said Michael Brown, a songwriter who knew her from parties, "in her incessant flow of words, in her Southernness. . . There was a tragic aura about Nina." Booze was where she found her relief. It consoled her, but it also caused "lightning rages" which Capote was forced to contend with at all hours of the day or night. Nina had little difficulty leaving Truman alone as a child, but that was no option for him when it came to her increasingly mordant, alcohol-abetted needs. Capote was on call around the clock. He was nominally a son, but he also functioned as therapist, a job he resented.

But if no one got under Truman's skin the way Nina did, no one focused his attention in quite the same way, either. In relation to her, he was never more than a child, chronically hungry for the affection and approval so searingly withheld. Now that she was gone, he'd never get it—at least not from her, the person who mattered most, despite what a disappointment she'd been. But death does not bring relationships to an end. Death is the birth of the image; the image endures as an internalized mental structure, a compound of ambivalence, resentment, disappointment, and grief. It keeps making demands, eliciting behaviors—but now these behaviors coalesce around new and different targets, substitute objects. Put simply, the loss-afflicted person reenacts dynamics formed early on, but does so with people who *stand in for* the person—in this case Nina—who set the dynamics in motion originally. The behavioral and emotional strategies Capote learned for dealing with Nina he extended, now, to others. In a phrase used once by Freud, Capote never stopped interacting with Nina; after her death he did so *in effigy*. He transferred his feelings for her onto suitable others. Some of these "others" were real people, women Capote got close to: others were fictional characters, the form-fitted Holly Golightlys that drift in and out of Capote's books and stories.

People cling to trauma; they get fixated by it. They symbolically repeat it, either compulsively (neurotically, to no salutary purpose) or in order to accomplish some fractional mastery. As Capote said, his mother was the "single worst person" in his life. That's because, among other reasons, her evil genius, crazy-making patterns set Capote up for a life that never quite succeeded in escaping her malevolent influence. She rumbled and clattered eternally, a restive poltergeist.

Parents are a person's most important emotional influence. They set the temperature. On that score Capote rolled snake eyes. But he also had his aunts, the colorful Faulks—Mary Ida, Callie, Jennie, and Sook—the family that raised him (and Lillie Mae, too). There was never any serious question of not taking Truman in. They were used to children; it was automatic. The house itself was a ramshackle place with a center hall, in a town, Monroeville, with dirt roads that threw up enormous clouds of dust in hot, dry weather. As a resident recalls, one could write his name on every mirror in the home by lunchtime. To folks in Monroeville, you were a Yankee if you lived anywhere north of Birmingham. It was just that simple.

At the Faulks', Truman slept alone, while his first cousin, Jennings Faulk Carter, laid dismal claim to a pallet on the floor. "Normally you'd put two boys in one bed in a room," Carter later explained, "but Sook and Jennie knew [Truman] didn't want to sleep with anybody. . . . They just sort of bent to his whims."

Apparently not always. Though Capote sometimes called his aunts "these marvelous Weird Sisters," and at other times "that bunch of old maids," they were anything but pushovers. They came from a hardy line of stock stretching back to the Civil War and its difficult aftermath, a fact Capote explored in his very last piece of writing, "Remembering Willa Cather." According to yet another aunt, Marie Rudisill, "We were brought up tough. When I came back from college, I worked." In the morning she swept sidewalks. She also swept Jennie's millinery shop on the square. "I wasn't allowed to play all summer," Rudisill says. "I was taught to work."

Mary Ida was tiny, a bantam rooster of a woman, and if something didn't go her way, according to one Monroeville acquaintance, "she would just lambast you up one side and down the other." But she was generous too, active in the community, prone to opening up her home to friend and relatives. In retirement age she purchased a motorcycle, roaring up into the Carolinas. Jennie was also gruff, short-tempered. She apparently liked Truman, enjoyed hearing him talk, but when the tales got too tall, she lost patience. "You're just lying, Truman, just get off that," was a common rejoinder. Jennie was the boss, no question about that; people "walked on tiptoes" when she was around. Arriving home from her shop at night, she would drop a canvas moneybag with change and "quite a few bills" on the main table. Her habit, before dinner, was to slink off towards a back closet where she kept her "medicine"—Ezra Brooks bourbon—which she downed in one gulp. Aunt Callie, weak in comparison to the other two women, was a complainer-type, sanctimonious to a fault, habitually assuming a defensive air of moral superiority.

Then there was Aunt Sook, pure Southern grotesque, hovering in the background. "She wasn't a mental elephant or anything like that," according to Rudisill, "but she lived in a dream world of her own devising,; her life lacked any reality. She wasn't particularly shy; she talked with guests at Sunday dinners. But she avoided going to town. She did her shopping on the telephone. She also didn't go to church, and according to Jennings Faulk Carter, the only movie she ever saw was *Gone with the Wind*, which she turned her nose up at because its account of the war wasn't "really like her daddy said it was." The film, she figured, ought to match her father's version of the history of the South. If she needed chewing tobacco, which was often, her favorite brand being Brown Mule, she sent Truman or Harper Lee up to town to get her a plug. Most people took Sook for a "retard," as they did Capote, before he put the lie to such ideas. In fact, she was introverted, unworldly, and nervous. Nina sent Capote clothes by mail, dressed him too well, made him more conspicuous than he already was; Sook took this one step further, outfitting Truman in ladies' clothes, enhancing his girliness, treating him like a doll. "There was the sense of being loved," Rudisill explained, "but it was not the right kind of love." Sook was, in Rudisill's view, "doing the wrong thing for [Truman]." The girls' clothes were part of the problem. She also forbade bicycle riding, for fear Capote might get hurt. "Just pampered, pampered," Rudisill said.

Capote stuck out in more ways than one, but the clothes certainly enhanced his already flagrant eccentricity. For games of tennis it was white linen shirts and pants, white socks, white shoes, even a white tie. At the swimming hole, kids stood around with their mouths wide open, gawking at Capote in "a dressmaker's swimsuit with a shirt and little tailored shorts.". He looked like "a bird of paradise in a flock of scrawny turkeys." Said one childhood friend, "It must have been real rough on him. He probably would have rather been wearing bib overalls and little khaki shorts like all the other boys." You just didn't touch his clothes, Carter recalled. He wore clean ones almost every day, unheard of in country children "because the wash is done by hand." The other boys tried dirtying him up, to no avail.

"Girliness" described Truman superficially—he was too fastidious, too self-enhanced—but kids learned not to discount his likewise freaky athleticism. He was very muscular. He out-chinned all the boys, and Harper Lee to boot. He climbed rope bare-handed.

He'd scale a rock fence around the Faulk home, four feet high, then execute a perfect cartwheel, something none of the other kids even dreamed of trying. At the same time, according to Carter, he never hit anybody; he'd never fight. For other children it was fists first, words later. For Truman it was words, always words. "My father had me take lessons from Jack Dempsey," he might say. "I could knock you out, but I won't." Then he'd cartwheel in the bully's face, leaving him awed or at least nonplussed.

He was also incredibly inventive and clever, his mind running at a fevered clip. He'd cobble together circuses and charge admission, exhibiting fake two-headed chickens he'd talk friends into building from scratch. The crowning event from this time was a Halloween costume party he spent weeks dreaming up, when he learned, in the second grade, that he'd be leaving Monroeville temporarily to head north with his mother. It was to take place on a Friday night—a rarity, since kids simply did not have nighttime parties. There were dozens of games, such as Chinese boxes Capote put together, each with a hole in the top. Kids guessed the contents; in one was a huge terrapin Capote turned on its back, others held mashed up oranges and bananas or turkey-wing dusters. Capote set up an incline kids zipped down in his Ford Trimotor pedal airplane.

The night also had its measure of controversy. Capote had arranged for Negro servants, one wearing a white hat, to supervise the apple-bobbing. (White hat notwithstanding, this particular worker apparently once had killed several people with his revolver.) Another was in charge of the records on the phonograph, which he flipped when necessary. The Ku Klux Klan got worked up; they planned to march down Alabama Avenue in front of Jennie's house, according to the sheriff, who always called Capote "Mr. Truman." Suddenly there was a commotion; the sheet-covered Klansmen had grabbed Sonny, a local recluse, the inspiration, according to Carter, for Boo Radley in Harper Lee's *To Kill a Mockingbird*. Mr. Lee (Harper's father) intervened, and the Klansmen slowly melted away, grinding their torches in the dirt.

The next morning, his Fu Manchu devil outfit tossed aside, Capote was all worked up, proclaiming the Klan dead. "Nobody will back them. We saw the Ku Klux Klan commit suicide." It was yet another instance, hardly the first or last, of Capote's always overactive imagination trumping reality utterly.

•　•　•

In 1971 Capote was asked by an interviewer, "If I say 'family,' what do you think?" His reply: "Well, I have many relatives. But *I would not say I have any family*. My family is what I consider just my friends."

This miasma of influences—a snake's nest of *No's* interrupted by very occasional *Yes's*—toughened Capote "rather too soon," he said, and forced him to develop "the muscles of a barracuda," but it also, and far less felicitously, forced the refinement of a personality style that caused as much trouble as it vanquished. Here it is necessary to formally introduce psychological research in personality as a means of making sense, a way of going beyond biographical fact to emotional subtext. Two models in particular shed special light on Capote's early experience: Silvan Tomkins's *script theory*, with its emphasis on affect (or emotion, feelings), scenes (discrete events or episodes), and the "scripts" (sets of rules) that evolve to interpret them; and *attachment theory*, especially its current iteration focused on adult manifestations of childhood attachment dynamics.

Already we've come across a handful of very important childhood scenes. Each warrants a prominent place in the jigsaw of Capote's unique psychology. There's the hotel room lock-in; the Busybody story; the IQ test; and Capote's memory of standing forlornly, like a neglected dog, watching his mother drive away in a black Buick, leaving him in the literal dust. Scenes like these are defined, technically, as *affect-laden happenings* (emotion-filled events), and they represent a fundamental unit-of-analysis—i.e., a slice of life-history information—in Tomkins's script theory. At a minimum, scenes contain one affect and one object of affect, although they can be far more complicated than that, too. Life itself is one very long procession of scenes. When we think about who we are, we think in scene terms. We tell stories. The self is a remembered thing. We are what we recall having said or done. And this kind of recollection, like all recollection, in fact, is a construction. It may be largely accurate, it may be fractionally embellished, it may be utterly fanciful. But whatever the case, scenes are the anchors around which we drift. They pin us to particular spots in the master narrative that is a life.

Not all scenes come to figure prominently. Some are trite, prosaic. Some slowly evaporate. Some are swiftly forgotten. The deciding factor is affect. For Tomkins, affect is everything. Seemingly the smallest, most inconsequential of events can take on fantastic meaning if invested with a density of affect; likewise, events that appear to be uniquely formative, especially powerful, slink away into perfect meaninglessness when not affect-heavy. Scenes are like boxcars. Their freight is feeling. The more packed the boxcar is, the more important its load. Empty boxcars don't get unpacked; full boxcars do, and the unloading can take a while.

So, one thing scenes do is tell us about a person's problematic affects or feelings, the kinds of emotions a person spends most of his time working through. For Capote, the four scenes described can be reduced to two pairs: the hotel room and the departing mother, and Busybody and the IQ test. For convenience, let's call the first pair "ouch" and the second pair "table-turning." What the "ouch" scenes do very effectively is summarize Capote's lifelong emotional setting: sadness, grief, abandonment fear, panic, and anger. The basic feature is *getting hurt*. And the affect's object is, of course, a colossally important attachment figure, a person who is needed, depended on, who is—for better or worse—in control, in a position of power: the mother or, in some versions of the hotel lock-in, the mother and the father.

The "table-turning" scenes are more complex. For them, the emotions are, in the end, positive rather than negative. There's interest, enjoyment, excitement. Capote feels puffed up, or as he put it, "proud." His personal power is on display, and the power revolves around his mind—its strength—and his talent, his writing. The affect's object, in this instance, is a conglomeration, a grouping. It's aimed at all those people who would doubt him, call him names, underestimate his abilities, misjudge his mettle. That's where "table-turning" comes in. He shows these people they were wrong about him. He's not just a "pocket Merlin"—as Harper Lee once called him—not some innocuous, insipid petite, but a barracuda. You best look out, these scenes say, because I'm no passive target. Diminish me and you'll pay.

At the highest level of Tomkins's system is the script. All scenes embed scripts; the script is the scene's bone structure, the skeleton. Scripts are like schemas or sets of rules. They are mini-theories of the self, unconsciously applied. In simplest terms, scripts bind together families of thematically similar scenes. They simplify and reduce complexity. Scripts are limitless in number; any life might contain dozens, but some—those invested with especially high quotas of affect—become dominant, super-powerful. They have an attracting quality; they colonize experience. They are self-validating and self-fulfilling.

For each of Capote's pairs of scenes—"ouch" and "table-turning"—a script can be extracted. If the scene is the boxcar and affect its cargo, the script is the train that pulls everything along. In "ouch" scenes, Capote's hopes get dashed. He's with his mother, his parents, the prized and coveted objects; he's expecting, perfectly reasonably, closeness, love, care, or at least responsiveness. Instead, he's rejected, abandoned; and he's bereft, hurt. Initial excitement leads to disappointment (not getting what he needs), and disappointment leads to despair. Something potentially good—for instance, his mother at last showing up in Monroeville, Alabama—turns woeful. "Table-turning" reverses this formula. Rejection by generalized others—neighbors, his family, teachers who call him "subnormal"— precipitates anger, strength, secret pride, and the outcome is a joyful repudiation, what psychologist Dan McAdams might call *redemption*. Doubt and rejection occasion a virtual godlikeness, a giddy "I told you so," or "Be careful who you mess with."

The truly amazing power of scene identification and script extraction is precisely this: scripts embedded in super-salient scenes become (hypothetically at first) organizing templates for the life in question. The script, when dominant, doesn't just capture the basic DNA of this one scene here; it also works for that one there, and many others to boot. It can be *extended*. The life adheres to the outline it provides. The script is the personality's *deep structure*.

Truman Capote, in so many aspects of his incredibly rich and varied life, remained at root either the sensitive, hurt boy or the barracuda. In fact, in wonderfully arresting fashion, the sensitive, hurt boy sometimes *elicited* the barracuda, and vice versa. In hurt-boy mode, Capote was quite direct: "There was a great absence of love in my childhood." He was "very sensitive and intelligent, [but] with no sense of being particularly wanted by anybody." He added: "The only way people can hurt me is if I let them get close to me. And sometimes I meet people who aren't what they make themselves out to be. Then I get hurt. But I'm very careful about that now, about who I get close to."

In 1980, an interviewer asked him: What, of your own experiences, have been the most frightening? "Betrayals. Abandonments," Capote replied. His *biggest* disappointments? "I believed people that I shouldn't have believed, that's about what it comes to. . . . And then, when it's something important, I get a real sinking feeling. That's happened several times in my life." Bingo. This is the "ouch" script in flagrant action. If you trust, if you believe, you get hurt. The interviewer asked, Can you be specific? Capote answered, "No"— the effect was just too hurtful.

The "ouch" script really was omnipresent. In 1970, when speaking with David Frost, Capote was reminded of an earlier statement he had made. Once, while discussing the possibility of psychotherapy, a prospect he seriously entertained on occasion, Capote imagined it might have "lessened the penalties I pay." Frost asked him what he meant by that. "I don't think it's possible to go through life," Capote replied, "without being continuously hurt one way or another. . . . If I feel somebody has betrayed me in some way about something, I get terribly upset."

By far the most precise expression of this core formula occurred when Capote zeroed in on the hotel room incident. He told biographer Gerald Clarke, "Every day was a nightmare, because I was afraid they would leave me when it turned dark. *I had an intense fear of being abandoned*, and I remember practically all of my childhood as being lived in a state of constant tension and fear."

So we return, yet again, to the scene we started with. What is obvious is that, even compared to other scenes like Busybody or the IQ test, the hotel lock-in is *unique*. It's super-potent. And when a scene achieves this sort of super-potency in a life, it rises, so to speak, to a prototypical status. It becomes a *prototypical scene*. How so? It expresses many of the core parameters of a person's life history. It assumes the status of a blueprint.

As I described them in another publication, prototypical scenes have the following features: They are emotionally "hot." They depict family conflict. They interpenetrate—they come up in a variety of contexts, fiction, art, letters, journals. They recur and metastasize. They also include an element of "thrown-ness." That is, they involve a violation of the status quo, a disruption in the normally taken-for-granted. Something unexpected is done to the person, and it throws him off kilter; it forces a coming to terms, a reckoning.

All these aspects converge in Capote's hotel room memory. It's hot, there's conflict with family (mother and father), the episode recurs, gets told again and again; it even assumes symbolic form in the fiction (as we'll see shortly and throughout this book). And it also constitutes a violation—children do not customarily expect to be locked away as their parents, those on whom they count and depend, party into the night. In this one scene, then, an enormous amount of psychological meaning is constellated and condensed. It is the life story writ small. As such, it's useful as a guide, a touchstone, as we continue exploring Capote's mental life.

There's more to say about the "table-turning" script, too. It governed Capote's dealings with perceived doubters, and because it worked to protect him against the pain that the doubt occasioned, it stayed on red alert. The word "perceived" is critical. Capote saw enemies where there actually *were* enemies; but he also saw them where they *weren't*. His life was haunted, with doubting poltergeists around every corner, whispering and snickering. Dealing with enemies, Capote said, was "an art no less necessary than knowing how to appreciate one's friends." When the IQ results came in, Capote was "exceedingly pleased—I went around staring at myself in mirrors and sucking in my cheeks and thinking over in my mind, my lad, you and Flaubert," geniuses both! His teachers refused to believe it, his family did not *want* to believe it—they'd hoped to be told he was simply a nice, normal boy. But he wasn't. He wasn't normal. And he wasn't necessarily nice, either. Any stimulus might, even under bewildering circumstances, fling him into attack mode.

Cataloguing instances of Capote's viciousness is a simple task. He called Joyce Carol Oates "the most loathsome creature in America," said "she ought to be beheaded in a public auditorium or in Shea [Stadium] or in a field with hundreds of thousands [watching]." As for John Updike? "I hate him. Everything about him bores me. He's like a piece of mercury, you put a drop in your hand and you try to hold onto it, you can't figure out what it's all about." What about erstwhile friend Tennessee Williams? "Here's a dumpy little guy with a dramatic mind who, like one of his adrift heroines, seeks attention and sympathy by serving up half-believed lies to total strangers." Capote even claimed, in barracuda mode, that he caused best-selling writer Jacqueline Susann's death. "She was lying in bed dying of cancer. I was on television and some-body asked me what did I think of Jacqueline Susann. And I said, 'She looks like a truck driver in drag.' She fell out of the bed. . . and never recovered. She sued me for a million dollars." The list goes on and on. Eugene O'Neill? "An untalented man." W.H. Auden? "A dictatorial bastard." Jack Kerouac? "Joke, Joke, Joke."

Capote always claimed to feel no envy at all, not the slightest twinge of competition with any other writer, living or dead. But there's an obvious peremptoriness to his attack impulse; the script, when activated, said "attack first, and don't ask questions later." He disparaged those he perceived, however vaguely, as rivals; but he really carved up anyone who did him wrong, or even threatened to do him wrong in some harrowing, undefined future.

Capote's most famous feud was with the writer Gore Vidal, another person who, like Tennessee Williams, had once been a close friend. In an interview in 1972, Capote was asked why the Kennedys turned against Gore. He repeated a story told to him by Jackie Kennedy's sister, Lee Radziwill, who said that Gore, at some official White House event, had put his hand on Jackie Kennedy's bottom as he strode out of a room. There was more: Vidal was drunk, Capote said. He insulted Jackie's mother. He'd been picked up and tossed out by guards. Vidal sued Capote for libel. The matter was settled out of court in 1983; Capote was forced to write an apology.

But Capote vs. Vidal was a tepid sideshow. The real heat came when Radziwill refused to testify in court on Capote's behalf, backing up Gore instead. "I don't recall ever discussing with Truman Capote the incident or the evening which I understand is the subject of this lawsuit," she told Gore's lawyer. It was a crushing, humiliating blow. Lee was one of Capote's "swans," a very dear friend, his "Galatea," according to Clarke. But now she refused to return his calls. And Capote went "totally berserk," in gossip columnist Liz Smith's words. The last straw, apparently, was Radziwill's vicious explanation—to Smith, not to Capote: "What does it matter? They're just a couple of fags."

Now, the Busybody/IQ script exploded. Capote had been dismissed, betrayed, waved off, in most repulsive fashion. Before he was a "retard," "subnormal." Now he was a "fag." The shit hit the proverbial fan. In perfect Busybody mode, Capote dusted off the blowtorch. "I'll tell you something about fags, especially Southern fags," he said in a TV interview. "We is mean. A Southern fag is meaner than the meanest rattler. . . . We just can't keep our mouths shut." Radziwill wanted to get in Bill Buckley's pants, he said. She'd plotted to marry Onassis herself. She had a crush on Jack Kennedy. She got dumped by lover Peter Beard when he "met this chick with a little less mileage on her." In short, Capote did what he always did in conditions of real or perceived betrayal: he bit back, and he bit hard, with the iron jaw of a pit bull.

· · ·

Attachment theory is the other indispensable framework for sizing up Capote's early life. This model was initially articulated by psychoanalyst John Bowlby, refined by Mary Ainsworth, and extended into the realm of adulthood by researchers such as Phil Shaver and Mario Mikulincer. It centers on the fundamental importance of relationships with significant others, with whom we form, from infancy, either affectional or attachment bonds. The latter are critical. We attach most firmly and come to rely most urgently on people whom we turn to for comfort and emotional reassurance in times of distress. These people are, of course, typically our parents, but not exclusively. Attachment hierarchies take shape over time. One's parents might be at the top of the list, but uncles, aunts, and others—in this case even friends like Harper Lee—can play important roles as well.

The goal of attachment is the regulation of emotion. We reduce fear, anxiety, anger, sadness, and emptiness by seeking out those who reliably respond to whatever needs emerge. This "seeking out" entails what is called *proximity-seeking*: staying close to and maintaining a bond with attachment figures. In the small child, proximity-seeking has literal meaning; in adults it can take the form of phone calls, texts, and other relatively symbolic forms of connecting. We evolve over time an attachment system, an internalized, abstract working model that refines itself incrementally; it works like an implicit theory of self in relation to others, and includes sets of expectations about how people are liable to react when we turn to them in times of distress. Will they respond, will they be available and capable of soothing fear, or will they reject us, ignore us? In short, can we count on important others?

Threats to availability and responsiveness are continuously appraised at an unconscious level. The attachment system gets intermittently activated, and when that occurs, different learned strategies emerge—we do what our past tells us works to draw out desired responses from those we depend on. These responses, functional or dysfunctional, become habitual, over-learned behaviors. They compose our particular, unique attachment style.

One can be *securely* attached, an optimal but relatively uncommon style. If secure, we know from our history that important others will be available and suitably responsive in times of need. Then there are the insecure attachment styles. One can be *anxiously* attached, prone to overestimating threats, on a sort of red alert, never quite sure others can be counted on, in a state of low-grade fear and uncertainty. And one can be *avoidantly* attached, habitually turning away from others and minimizing threats defensively out of fear that approach—proximity-seeking—will lead to rejection or hostility or betrayal. By now an impressively massive amount of experimental research exists concerning the life outcomes of these three main styles. The degree to which these styles correlate with other personality constructs such as extraversion, neuroticism, and openness (to name just a few) is also clear. In simplest terms, if a person's attachment style can be assessed, the results of that assessment tell us a lot about that person's moods, tendencies, defenses, thinking patterns, and most important, motives for relating with others.

Attachment is a lifespan model. Patterns take shape in early childhood but extend into adulthood. They persist. They determine adult feelings, needs, and behaviors. What Shaver and Mikulincer have convincingly shown is that anxiously attached children become *hyperactivating* adults; avoidant children become *deactivators*. What does this mean, exactly? Adults who make use of hyperactivating attachment-related strategies *intensify emotion* as a means of eliciting responses; they sustain and exaggerate fear, sadness, anger, anxiety, and rage. They "up-regulate" threat appraisals. The smallest signs of rejection or even simple disinterest are magnified. Helplessness, neediness, and vulnerability get overemphasized because these, in the past, have worked to mobilize attention and care. Hyperactivators are chronically clingy, needy, emotionally labile, and supersensitive. Their demands on others are intense. They crave intimacy, flagrantly advertising negative emotion until they get it; and when they get it, they fear letting go.

Deactivators are mirror-opposites. They aim to block, suppress, or *inhibit emotional states* associated with threat-related thoughts or perceptions. For them, negative emotion signals weakness, so they simply do not feel; they practice obliviousness, and they develop an exaggerated self-reliance, a compulsive independence.[1] They need no one (or so they claim). They are the expert avoiders of the world. They refuse to problem-solve (they deny all problems), they have a hard time evaluating emotions (no practice at it), and they come to doubt the general goodness of the world, since counting on others has only gotten them hurt.

I prolong this particular discussion of the nuts and bolts of theory for one key reason: attachment is a powerful lens with which to zero in on Capote's psychological life. It's an ideal template we can superimpose on the particulars of his sense of self and others,

---

1. The comment, "they simply do not feel," requires some explanation. Lack of feeling is what deactivators *profess*. In fact, at deep physiological levels, deactivators respond with increased arousal and anxiety when questioned about attachment history.

even his art. It does not tell us everything we need to know—nothing will do that—but it's a strikingly effective organizing superstructure on which to base some initial formulations.

First things first. Capote was insecurely attached. His parents were generally unavailable and unresponsive to his needs—that much is obvious. There was, as he said succinctly, an *absence of love*. He had his aunts, but his attitude towards them was ambivalent; they raised him, they took on that responsibility, but Capote felt little closeness, except towards Sook. But Sook was a child, not a grownup. She could hardly be counted on in times of distress. In 1932, Nina did swoop in and bring Truman with her to her new home in New York City, where he attended a private Episcopal school for boys on the West Side of Manhattan, but her focus was on café society, parties, and social climbing. If she paid him any attention, it was to express disapproval—his homosexuality was a serious problem for her. She condemned, in other words, a central aspect of who he was. And when she was drinking, good Nina turned into bad Nina with "terrifying speed," according to Clarke. After months of conflict and frustration and a handful of meetings with psychiatrists, Nina made the preposterous decision to send Truman to military school. The uniform of the cadet might make him manly, she figured. His homosexuality would be drilled out of him. No such luck. In fact, his size and prettiness made him catnip for older boys, who steered Truman into their beds after lights out. "They took sex very seriously," Capote recalled later. "Instead of making me happy and secure, being chased after like that had the opposite effect." He said it was like prison, and he was "the pretty convict" everyone went after.

The insecurity of Capote's attachment is evident. The next question's more complicated. Generally speaking, deactivation and hyperactivation function antithetically. One amps up emotion, one buries it. But Capote experienced both *rejection* (associated with deactivation) and *unresponsiveness* (associated with hyperactivation)— so he evolved alternating strategies, triggered according to the exact situation. In school, for instance, he threw tantrums easily, dropping to the floor and kicking his legs and screaming. He was labeled "disturbed." But the behavior had a purpose. It advertised his pain and elicited consoling reactions. On the other hand, he could deny hurt, too. He said, "I was loved by my mother and father, but I never saw them"—a glaring contradiction, as if love and invisibility were anything but mutually exclusive. He also, in deactivating mode, had a tendency to trumpet his toughness. No one bothered him. He cared little what anyone thought. He was immune.

When Capote says he had "no family, only friends," the comment makes sense when seen from the viewpoint of attachment. His friends *were* his attachment figures. He got close to *them*. They shored him up. If he wanted, Clarke says, he could charm almost anyone. It was a talent he evolved and relied on increasingly—it drew others close, it made them pay attention. "It was fascinating to watch him," a childhood friend said. Truman might tag along to parties in a tuxedo. The boys there immediately gravitated to him, expecting instant entertainment. The elaborate games, the fantastical scenarios other kids playacted, the cartwheels, the jaw-dropping acrobatics—all these skills were life-savers. They galvanized attention. They elicited the sorts of approving reactions in such short supply elsewhere. And they extended into adulthood. Physical acrobatics were replaced by the verbal variety. As an adult, whether writing or appearing on talk shows, Capote captivated with words. People came near simply to hear what he had to say. His wit, sarcasm, and apparently fearless flamboyancy almost never failed him.

3 | LEAVING THE BOY BEHIND?

Capote wouldn't have minded psychobiography. In fact, he was a believer, at least by implication. To Capote, the truly great writers projected their personality at once. It was there in the work, "like a character that makes contact with the reader." He thought long and hard about matters of style, concluding that "your style *is* you," no more consciously arrived at than "the color of one's eyes." And if the personality was vague or confused or merely literary? That was a big problem.

Capote distrusted psychoanalysis, in part because of his history of confrontation with Nina over matters of sexuality, her willingness to turn to doctors when seeking solutions for his girliness. Her sense, misguided in the extreme, was that talk therapy might "make him a man." No such luck. At any rate, Capote was clear: he dealt with his problems in his work. It was in his writing that he understood and defined himself. And this process began with his very first published book, *Other Voices, Other Rooms*, a slightly scandalous and not entirely successful homosexual fantasia, in which Capote replayed attachment anxieties like those described already, but in the process also tried leaving the boy from Monroeville behind.

Capote used to say he carried a whip for self-flagellation; if so, he used it often when working on *Other Voices*. The strain was terrific, his expectations so high he constantly feared failure (as most artists do). "I do not take to this brand of pressure," he wrote in 1947. "Every word takes blood." Still, at around the same time he called the book "really my love," telling a friend, "I do want it to be a beautiful book because it seems important to me that people try to write beautifully, now more than ever because the world is so crazy and only art is sane." This statement neatly encapsulates Capote's basic attitude. Art was where he found clarity, where he assumed complete control; everything else was "madness."

When writing *Other Voices*, and even for many years afterwards, Capote avoided its emotional meaning and the way it insidiously enfolded so many of his most difficult conflicts. Rereading it later, perturbed by his "adamant ignorance," he found such self-deception unpardonable, though obviously protective. The writer, he said, sometimes needs to place a "fire curtain" between himself and the true source of his material. Lacking such a compartmentalization, books sometimes do not get written. The writer can be waylaid by his own complicated prehistory, or what Capote described as "the anxieties that then had control of my emotions and imagination." With hindsight, he could afford a different view, and what he saw was unmistakable. The book was an attempt to exorcise demons, and an "unconscious, altogether intuitive attempt," at that. It was the message of a shipwrecked sailor "stuffed into a bottle and thrown into the sea." Its progenitor was Capote's difficult, subterranean self. The result "was both a revelation and an escape: the book set me free. . . . I stood there and looked back at the boy I had left behind."

I am not so certain the book succeeded at that. I am also not so certain Capote was ever set free from his anxieties, or that he really left anything behind. There is an important difference between unconsciously disguised *expression* and *restitution*, though the two get confused all the time. I believe in art's power and potential, but writing is never intrinsically, automatically therapeutic. It can be a little (or a lot) crazy-making, too. What Capote did with *Other Voices* was important, but more modest. He crafted what he called a "prose-poem" that set his conflicts down for all who looked hard enough to see. It was an intuitive confession. It was cathartic. It amounted to a self-psychobiography. On its heels there arrived almost instant fame, of the sort one no longer sees afforded literary figures (sadly). But Capote was not profoundly altered. He was not "liberated." His childhood was just as haunting and demon-littered as ever. That particular reality never changed. As Capote's longtime lover Jack Dunphy put it, the "sting of broken promises" never left Truman. He talked to Nina even in his sleep.

The young Joel Knox is *Other Voices'* hero. And in that he is too pretty, fair-skinned, delicate, girlishly tender, and smart—speaking words most folks in Noon City, the book's setting, never heard said—he is also obviously Truman. As Joel declares at one point: "I'm thirteen, and you'd be surprised how much I know." This is Capote in the IQ-script mode. Joel might benefit from some "mussing up," as one character suggests, but at least he's a genius. Geniuses can do some mussing up of their own. He also tells really good lies—just like Capote in Busybody mode, except that Joel's lies tend to be of the harmless variety.

But the book's central theme revolves around attachment. His mother having passed away, and living now with his aunt, Joel receives a letter from one Edward R. Samson, the father he has not seen since infancy. Samson wants Joel back. He plans to assume paternal duties, "forsaken, lo, these many years." The setup is pure wish-fulfillment. Capote conjures a father who desires him, who wants to set things right, make up for lost time, an anti-Arch. So Joel heads out hopefully for Noon City. It's a rough trip through lonesome country, with logs shining under marsh water like drowned corpses. The farmhouses are sorry-looking, the birds wing-stiffened, the buildings thrown together haphazardly "by a half-wit carpenter." Immediately one gets the strong sense that things are not what they seem. This will be no happy family reunion. Is there even a father at all?

The people Joel meets along the way are equally disconcerting, a menagerie of strangeness. There's Jesus Fever, a derby-wearing pygmy; there's Idabel Thompkins, a fiery androgyne with dutchboy hair and a talent for twisting her face into evil shapes; there's Zoo, Jesus Fever's grandchild, a childlike, simpleminded cook obsessed with a need to see snow, resembling, in many respects, Capote's aunt Sook; and most importantly of all, there's Cousin Randolph, a Southern-fried Oscar Wilde. Randolph is essentially a failure, a drunk, a recluse. Up close he emits a delicate lemon scent; he wears seersucker kimonos with butterfly sleeves; his exposed toenails reveal a manicured gloss. From time to time he doles out little paradoxical Wildean epigrams, as when he soberly asks Joel, "Have you never heard what the wise men say? All of the future exists in the past."

Maybe strangest of all is the "queer lady" Joel spies twice behind a corner window of his father's home. She smiles and nods, her "towering pale pompadour" dribbling fat curls. Her presence puts the world in a trance. Butterflies pause; rasping bumblebees silence themselves.

The first half of the book is a mystery tale. Joel reaches The Landing, meets Zoo, Randolph, and Miss Amy (his father's new wife), but can't seem to get anyone to tell him anything about his father, or who or where he is. Everyone he asks changes the subject, or answers allusively. Joel is on a hero's quest. What he's after is a father's love, just like Truman. Capote interestingly prolongs Joel's pain, subjects him to emotional torture, as if repeating his own paralysis. Joel keeps telling himself, "Dad will probably want me in a minute," but on the other hand he's not so sure; maybe he's been "played a mean trick." Zoo suggests that he pray. He asks for a bicycle, a knife with seven blades, a box of oil paints. But such requests seem indefinite, meaningless. Finally Joel speaks to God a sentence straight out of Capote's life: "Let me be loved."

It's a prayer ignored. *Other Voices* essentially adheres to Capote's "ouch" script. He seeks love, he tries to make himself as lovable as possible, but what he finds is hurt, disappointment, and betrayal. Even God Joel does not much like: "He had betrayed him too many times." Joel's father finally does the same. It's not until page 121 that the boy lays eyes on Samson[1]. And the sight is infinitely sorry. His head is shaved. He lies "with invalid looseness on unsanitary pillows." His eyes search Joel with a "kind of dumb glitter." In short, he's helpless. His needs he communicates by feebly tossing a red tennis ball down the stairs. Joel gamely tries reading to him, he tries connecting, but Samson never listens. Prices recited from a Sears Roebuck interest Samson as much as the best wild-west story.

From the standpoint of attachment, it's impossible to imagine a clearer depiction of attachment-figure unresponsiveness. Capote really piles it on. Even words, his *métier*, fail to raise a pulse in the object of his desire; they carry no thrilling meaning. Joel/Truman can't win. There is no love anywhere, no sense of whom or what to

---

1. An interesting name choice. The biblical figure Samson is Herculean, granted tremendous strength by God. He wrestles lions, slays armies with a donkey's jawbone, and smashes temples. This is the kind of father Capote's limitless imagination concocted; but his Samson is anything but Samsonlike.

blame. Joel feels "separated, without identity, a stone-boy mounted on a rotted stump."

From here, the book, its mystery revealed, crawls episodically and far less compellingly towards a finish line. Joel runs away with Idabel. They find themselves at a carnival. Idabel, like Cousin Randolph, turns out to be gay—she falls for Miss Wisteria, a 25-year-old midget just back from a grand tour of Europe where she had appeared before all the crowned heads in silver slippers and a drape of purple silk. Joel gets caught up with but he's very sick; he spends dozens of pages in a hallucinatory fever.

Capote always aimed to pack a lot of meaning into the book's ending. Writing it was pure anguish. He couldn't say why, he noted, "especially since I know exactly what I'm doing." He told an aspiring young writer, "the 'secret' of the book, the meaning (and it has one), lies in the last few pages. I don't intend to tell you what it is, for someday you will see it for yourself. You do not yet know quite enough about life—."

The secret, in fact, remains obscure. Capote felt a need, perhaps entirely literary, to posit some sort of redemption. Joel declares, "I am me, I am Joel, we are the same people"—but it's far from obvious who this "we" includes. By now Samson is all but forgotten, an undemanding memory. He has gone back where he always was; he has become Arch. So Joel chooses Randolph, the one who actually wrote the letter, the one who really requested him (as it turns out). He could never quarrel with Randolph, he realizes, "for anger seemed, if anything, more unsafe than love." His mind suddenly clear, Joel catches sight of the queer lady again; this time she's in Randolph's window. She beckons, "shining and silver," and he knows he must go, "unafraid, not hesitating." The lady and Randolph are one and the same. What Joel/Truman avows is his true self, the part his mother never accepted. He confesses his homosexuality, casting a backwards glance "at the boy he had left behind."

Two other facts about Randolph make him an interesting choice as father-figure. Like Nina tried to make Truman do, Randolph attempted heterosexuality; he made himself want a woman named Dolores, but fell instead for Dolores's lover, Pepe. Pepe turned out to be a disappointment. Still, as Randolph intones in yet another moment of Wildean reverie, "Any love is beautiful and natural that lies within a person's nature"; only hypocrites, "emotional illiterates," and those of righteous envy would hold a man responsible for what he loves; people such as these "mistake so frequently the arrow pointing to heaven for the one that leads to hell." Capote, in other words, made of Randolph a consoling philosopher, a campaigner on behalf of "the love that dares not speak its name."

Also, with a nimbly executed symbolic flourish, Capote found Randolph responsible for Joel's father's invalidism, his unresponsiveness. While in a fit of romantic anguish, Randolph shot Samson, mistaking him for someone else. His homosexuality—beautiful and natural, something he was powerless to stop—silences Samson. The gay male slays the giant.

By now it is crystal clear why Capote, in retrospect, saw the book as "seriously" autobiographical, why he called it an exorcism. But there is more, other patterns even he may have missed. Attachment history—as we have seen—gives rise to learned behaviors, different forms of emotion regulation, perceptual set-points of hypervigilance or denial. But one aspect of psychological life *not* commonly tied to attachment, at least not to date, is creativity. Art is, among numberless other things, a form of thought. As such, it will also include attachment-driven preoccupations. And *Other Voices* does just this, in spades.

The relationships in the book repeatedly depict identical patterning. Zoo and Joel bond quickly. She is a source of comfort. Joel at one point tells her, gushingly, "I love you because you've got to love me because you've got to"—an oddly desperate plea, but understandable in light of Capote's life history. But, predictably, Zoo runs off, for Washington, D.C., where the snow is. Joel gives love; Joel is forsaken. Joel's strategy—like Capote's was, on occasion—is deactivation. He suppresses emotion and tells Zoo: "You're awful funny. You were never my friend. But after all why should anyone such as me have anything in common with such as you?" Even the language sounds stilted, false. Then, just as with Capote's memory of watching his mother drive off in the black Buick, Joel watches Zoo head down the road, "until she grew pinpoint small."

The same thing happens with troublemaking tomboy Idabel, who runs off with Joel, only to leave him for the midget, Wisteria. This time Joel is stuck on a Ferris wheel, watching it all unfold. Earlier Joel had, with "breathtaking delicacy," kissed Idabel's cheek. He had wanted to tell her, "I am your good true friend"; he'd wanted to touch her. It was the "only means of expressing all he felt." But the gesture—honest, vulnerable—caused Idabel to tighten. She yanked Joel's hair, and a "puzzled rage" ripped through him. This, Joel declares, "was the real betrayal." They fight, Joel bleeds, and Idabel informs him, "You'll be all right"—"as if nothing had happened. And, indefinably, it was as if nothing had." Joel lies: "I never cry." Another suppression of emotion.

Capote tips his hand about the capriciousness of love and its transitoriness before the book even begins. He cites Jeremiah 17:9: "The heart is deceitful above all things, and desperately wicked. Who can know it?" Definitely not Joel. Messages like this emerge with striking frequency. Capote speaks them out loud, like hard-won, hard-earned life lessons. For instance: "It was unsafe ever to let anyone guess the extent of your feelings or knowledge. . . . If concealment is the single weapon, then a villain is never a villain: one smiles to the very end." And: "Human beings. . . . They could go right off the face of the earth. That was what happened to his father. So why did they pretend? Why didn't they say right out, 'There is no Mr. Samson, you have no father,' and send him on his way?" And his aunt, the woman who cared for Joel after his mother died? "The hell with her. He didn't care anymore. . . . And she'd made so many promises. And she'd said she loved him. But she forgot. All right, so had he, sure, you forget, ok, who cares?"

Expressions like these can be left unexamined, assigned a purely literary value—they work in the story, they help flesh out characters. And besides, Joel is not exactly Truman. He is a fiction. But even Capote felt otherwise. It's the job of the psychobiographer to keep an eye on the art's subjective origins, the way it expresses hidden motives or evolved psychological functions. In *Other Voices*, his first novel, Capote told his story. Like a lot of first novels do, the book sprang from the life; the life was its raw material. In general terms— boy goes in search of father, but finds feeble, helpless Samson—and more specifically, boy reaches out for love, only to be repeatedly rebuffed, Capote replayed his past. There was "always trickery in one hand, and danger in the other. No chance whatsoever. None." Joel copes the same way Capote did: by not feeling, by being brave, by never crying, by denying he had ever offered his love in the first place, by pretending not to care when he is left alone to fend for himself. Not always, but definitely in this particular instance, Capote invested in *deactivation*. He will not be hurt. He will not trust. He is bullet-proof. But even here, he also included a little spasm of *hyperactivation*, explaining that, on the occasions when affection was withheld from him, "he knew with what ease it could be guaranteed: a smile, a wistful glance, a courtly compliment." Capote was one of those rare birds who moved between strategies. When love was unlikely, he cut off emotion; when love was in his grasp, he made himself lovable. We will see these dynamics again. With *Answered Prayers*, they laid a foundation that then spun off into full "table-turning" frenzy.

We can leave *Other Voices* behind now, except for one final detail. The book was dedicated to Newton Arvin. As it turns out, that decision carries psychological weight.

Arvin was Capote's lover at the time he wrote the book. The two had been introduced by a man, Howard Doughty, who was also Capote's lover—and Arvin's! As Capote and Arvin's romance heated up, Doughty and Arvin's cooled down. Doughty professed, gallantly, not to care, thought it seems he did care more than he let on. For several years in the late 1940s, Capote and Arvin swooned mutually. To Capote, Arvin was simply "too good for me, too thoughtful; too kind: I am only glad that I am capable of appreciating him, and knowing his rarity, his delicate perfection." But as usual, love came fearfully: "Did you ever," Capote asked a friend, "in that wonderful wilderland of adolescence ever . . . see something . . . so exquisite [that] terror touched you at the bone? And you are afraid, terribly afraid the smallest movement . . . will shatter all? That is, I think, the way love is, or should be: one lives in beautiful terror." Did Capote ever live any other way, when it came to his affections?

Arvin was, if anything, even more effusive. He diligently read up on Capote's work to date, finding it lovely, frightening, pure, and tender, "like something seen suddenly and magically by snowfall." He gushed, "It would not be possible, it seems to me, for me to cherish you more tenderly, with more of myself, than I already do, but if it were possible, the reading of your stories would have that effect. Where did you come from, Truman?"

We know the answer to that question. But what about Arvin? Where did *he* come from? Smith College, most directly. He taught literature there for 38 years, and was a singularly talented literary critic, with books on Hawthorne, Whitman, Melville, and Longfellow. Alfred Kazin called Arvin's Melville work, in particular, the "wisest and most balanced single piece of writing on Melville I have seen." Capote was self-taught. He faked sickness as a boy in order to stay home and read. Books were his real best friend. But he lacked a classical education. Arvin made up for that. Arvin was Capote's college. There were times he sat in the back of Arvin's class, soaking up the erudition. And as he labored through *Other Voices'* final pages, he read Arvin sections of the work, which Arvin lightly revised.

Capote was 22 when he met Arvin, 23 years his lover's junior. And Arvin was a bit of a mess: depressed, fearful, reclusive, vertigo-afflicted. He had tried suicide three times and was hospitalized for assorted breakdowns. His father resembled Nina, always calling Newton a sissy. Crushingly, he refused to allow Arvin's mother to attend his Harvard graduation.

Largely on account of his father's critical judgments, no doubt, Arvin was ashamed of his sexuality. In 1932 he married a student, Mary Garrison. As Clarke notes, she was a little like Capote, at least temperamentally—outgoing, vivacious, resilient. They divorced in 1940, with Arvin bemoaning his "affectional impotence." "Every capacity for tenderness is present," he wrote, "except the one power of penetrating or being penetrated with the last intimacy." Something kept him from giving himself over. He needed solitude more than he needed people. Lacking it, he felt as if something physical were ebbing out of him, "like blood."

Joel may not have found a father in *Other Voices*, but Capote did in Arvin. The life, in a sense, improved on the fiction. The age difference between Arvin and Arch was a scant three years. They also looked alike: both balding, both thickly bespectacled. And Arvin worried over Capote with a peculiarly parental concern, "fretting like an old woman" on occasions when Capote went on assignment for magazines like *Harper's Bazaar*. Even the names "Edward Samson" and "Newton Arvin" share a syllabic affinity.

Other Voices' most convoluted signifier by far is Cousin Randolph. I suspect there is a bit of Arvin in him. Randolph, like Arvin, is reclusive, fearful, "solemn and baby-eyed," emotionally unhinged, in retreat from the world. When Arvin writes Capote to say, "I'm not a bad boy, and neither are you. . . for we are the source of good, and we are drinking the water of truth, and what we are making between us is purely beautiful," the speechifying sounds positively Randolphish. Randolph even tried marriage once before embracing his true nature with Pepe, just as Arvin did with Mary Garrison. Unconsciously, when Joel surrenders to Randolph and to homosexuality, Capote imagined a solution secured by Arvin's devotion.

And so, in short, the book's dedication makes sense. Arvin was wrapped up in it on many levels. Art held the mirror up to life. Though he always talked like a man obsessed, Arvin chose solitude over partnership; he led Capote on, then let him down, canceling one assignation after another out of fear of what others might think. Capote broke down, asked friends to cuddle and hold him and tell him everything would be all right. Then, utterly characteristically, with a resilience and independence specific to the deactivated style, he announced, "Never be without a novel. There are moments when you need one."[2]

---

2. Newton Arvin's eventual fate was miserable. In 1960, he was arrested for possession of homosexually themed pictures, charged with being "a lewd person." He pled guilty, paying fines of $1200. Police claimed Arvin led them to a colleague as well, and that both implicated other male faculty members (though Arvin's nephew denied this). Arvin was

There is one sense in which *Other Voices* was an exorcism: never again did Capote fashion a fictional father figure. From here on out, it was girls, girls, girls (and killers, the subject of the next chapter). And the first girl he turned to, the one he later called his favorite character, was Holiday Golightly ("Holly," for short). Perhaps unsurprisingly, there is a fair amount of Lillie Mae in Holly, and in the long list of mysterious, doomed female characters Capote featured in so many of his early stories. I think there is a fair amount of Capote in these women, too. They form a packed, psychologically layered hybrid. Getting at their emotional meaning requires some serious unwrapping.

Other Voices was Capote's father-dirge; ten years later came *Breakfast at Tiffany's*, the mother side of the coin. The book is a case study, far slighter than *Other Voices*, less intent on being beautiful. Its modest purpose is to portray "fragile eyeful" Holly, whose calling card lists her occupation as "Traveling." It is true—she does not stay put. She is a wild thing who cannot be trapped, let alone loved. Before noon she might have downed three Manhattans. Now and then she gets the urge to steal something at Woolworth's—"just to keep my hand in." Her brownstone crawls with men she's blithely enchanted, though none of them interest her much. Her actual age is 18; she strikes the nameless narrator as anywhere between 16 and 60. In a lot of ways—and this is one of the things that drew Capote to the character—Holly is a cipher. There is no core. Her childhood, when she is forced to recall it churlishly, is nameless, placeless, impressionistic. The narrator, whom Holly christens

suspended from teaching, and shortly afterwards hospitalized for suicidal depression. He died in 1963 of pancreatic cancer. "The last time I saw Newton," Capote wrote in 1960, "I rather thought that sex had taken over."

"Fred," after her brother, can't get her out of his mind. He's charmed by her, yet he detests her.

What seems to have been most on Capote's mind, more even than Holly herself, was *personality*—a subject that always enthralled him, for reasons having mainly to do with self-survival. He was interested in questions of nature versus nurture, of how identity both remains intact and refines itself: in other words, the mystery of how people change and stay the same, simultaneously. It is a subject that vexes personality researchers today. And it was no small matter for Capote. His life was devoted to carefully and effectively sizing up important others in order to get what he needed from them. Of necessity, he became adept at people-reading. He quickly figured what they were worth to him, and he learned when and how to make necessary withdrawals.

Holly, however, is an anomaly. Capote announced, "The average personality reshapes itself frequently . . . desirable or not, it is a natural thing that we should change." But Holly doesn't. In this way she defies the usual logic of storytelling: she's a main character who learns nothing, who stays the same. She was given her personality too soon, Capote said, just like he was. That led, like sudden riches will, to a lack of proportion. She became a "lopsided romantic." Holly is fated to "walk through life and out of it with the same determined step that took small notice of those cliffs at the left." She's oblivious, she won't learn; Capote finds this maddening, but admirable. She's another of his free spirits who refuses to let the world daunt her: "I am who I am, the world be damned. Take me or leave me."

Most people haven't read *Breakfast at Tiffany's*. They have seen the 1961 film. Their "Holly" is Audrey Hepburn, with her wide black hat, her cat named "Cat," and her ludicrously oversized (but iconic) cigarette holder, which in the movie poster matches the length of Holly's entire upper torso. It's too bad. The movie's Holly is nowhere near Capote's. Capote labeled the film a "mawkish Valentine"; the book, in contrast, was "really rather bitter." "[The movie] made me want to throw up," Capote said. "It's the most miscast film I've ever seen." Hepburn "was not who Holly *is*," Capote explained. Holly was not chic or lean or "bone-faced"; she was smart, but "in a totally different way": wily, resourceful, a schemer, running on guile and intuition. When talk of a remake surfaced, Capote suggested Jodie Foster, a far better fit (tough, pretty, self-surviving). But even at the time of the original, his first choice, an interesting one, was Marilyn Monroe.

"I met her in New York when Paramount was making the movie," said Truman. "I had seen her in a film and thought she would be perfect for the part. Holly had to have something touching about her, something . . . unfinished. Marilyn had that. But Paramount double-crossed me and gave the part to Audrey Hepburn."

Monroe, Capote felt, was really "very, very shy, very insecure," ostensibly like Holly, but then also "very, very bright, very perceptive." Marilyn "wasn't fooled by many people, and they thought [wrongly] that they were fooling her all the time." Still, there was no getting around the fact that "she was emotionally about eleven years old."

It's clear that Holly—and Marilyn—were working on a lot of different levels simultaneously. She's insecure, bright, perceptive, and won't be fooled—exactly like Truman. She's tortoise-shelled, a fighter—also like Truman. But Nina's in there, too. She's naïve, gullible, a crude exhibitionist, a time-waster, an "utter fake." And she refuses to learn. The world can't alter her because she takes no notice of it.

The plot, pretty slight, reduces to Fred chasing Holly, who remains unconscious of his existence. She can take him or leave him. She can take or leave anybody, in fact. He studies the trash-basket outside her door, reading its contents for clues (she survives on cottage cheese and melba toast, for one). She visits a mobster in Sing Sing, "Sally Tomato," who gives her messages to leave with an answering service, oblique sentences like *There's a hurricane in Cuba* or *It's snowing in Palermo*. These are codes with which Tomato, from prison, keeps first-hand control of a narcotics syndicate spanning at least five countries. Holly is arrested but flees to Brazil, maybe even Africa—no one is certain—never to be seen again.[3]

Stylistically, *Other Voices* was clotted, engorged, at times almost hallucinatory in its warped stylings and strivings. It's a precocious book, young, full of the overreaching symptomatic of impatience and ambition (e.g., "beneath the still façade of forest restless feet trampled plushlike moss where limelike light sifted to stain the natural dark"). Capote said the person who wrote it did not exist anymore. He's a stranger. *Tiffany's* he saw as his second career. The prose is pruned, thinned-out, subdued, clearer; the pyrotechnics nonexistent. The result may be less evocative, less original-seeming, but it was "harder to do." Style epitomizes different psychological attitudes: *Other Voices* convolutedly comes clean (although if you aren't paying attention, you might miss the message); *Tiffany's* is a clearheaded, clear-eyed dissection.

---

3. The movie is a treacly mess, though pretty to look at. It does not waste any time. It begins unimaginatively, with Holly stepping out of a cab after a long night partying, coffee and donut in hand, to *literally* have breakfast at Tiffany's. A few other oddities: Holly's from Texas but she speaks with an English accent; the movie gives the narrator a name that sounds like a punch in the face—"Paul Varjak"—and he's also published a book titled *Nine Lives*. Invented out of whole cloth is a "decorator" with whom Paul is having an affair (she disappears from the story); and the ending is total Hollywood. Paul delivers a speech to Holly, telling her she'll always be alone unless she lets herself be loved, unless she lets herself "belong to" someone. Her face shows an epiphany. She hops out of a cab, heaves her cigarette to the left, and kisses Paul in the pouring rain as "Moon River" drools out of the sky.

What everyone wanted to know—style aside—was who Holly was. Was she real? Was she fantasy? Who might claim credit or pride of origin? The fracas was a little like the one that ensued when *Answered Prayers* began appearing, also in serialized form, except then denials were the order of the day; no one wanted to *be* the characters portrayed, or in spitting distance of them. With *Breakfast at Tiffany's*, for odd reasons, *everyone* wanted to be Holly.

Capote's friend James Michener had his theory. He recalled a girl half of New York City was smitten by, himself and Capote included. Both of them took her on dates now and then, Capote apparently platonically. She was an Amazonian six feet two inches tall, a mountain next to Capote's molehill. Michener described her comically as a "stunning would-be starlet-singer-actress-raconteur from the mines of Montana," with "minimum talent, maximum beauty, and a rowdy sense of humor." So certain was Michener of Holly's derivation that when a different woman sued Capote out of nowhere—not the first, not the last—claiming to have been the model for Miss Golightly, Michener wrote the publisher, Random House, disputing her allegations. Capote asked him to destroy the letter. He worried the massive Montanan might sue too.

Others were less sure of the Montanan provenance. Gossip maven Doris Lilly nominated herself. "There's an awful lot of me in Holly Golightly, much more of me than there is of Carol Marcus [another candidate] and a girl named Bee Dabney, a painter [yet another candidate]. More of me than either of those two ladies. I know."

Other possible models included Anky Larabee (whom Capote met in 1946 and called entertaining, "slightly crazy," and sweet); Phoebe Pierce; Oona O'Neill; Gloria Vanderbilt—in short, virtually any partially or entirely upper-crust party girl who did her own thing and never looked back. It is amusing that so many women wanted to be Holly, the naïve narcissist. She's lovable and diverting, but that's about it. If you needed a true friend when the stakes were high and the odds were low, she was the last person you'd ring. Capote pictured her as the prototype of the late 1960's liberated female. Her disinhibition and lack of fear he regarded as "a damn good thing." She was also a more specific symbol—of a type of girl who came to New York at the time, who was ubiquitous in certain circles, and who "spun in the sun for a moment like May flies and then disappeared." These girls were not exactly prostitutes (though they could easily be mistaken for that). They were escorts only, therefore innocent and chaste, authentic American geishas. Sociologically, Capote wished to capture their ephemeral existence, to get them in their native habitat. So Holly was made to personify the type.[4]

Miss Golightly was a lot of people, a lot of things—at root, Capote's most prized invention. A Jodie Foster, a Marilyn Monroe, a refugee, an Amazon, a gossip girl, a geisha. In *Other Voices* Capote intentionally—but unconsciously—formulated a father saga that left him fatherless but self-aware, self-knowing, and set on his course of life. In *Tiffany's* he did the same. He conjured a mother whom he tries to love, *does* love, but who is not lovable, who won't stick around, who disappears forever—to Africa, no less.

Make no mistake: Holly is very Lillie-Mae derived. I have already alluded to her naïveté, her narcissism, her smarts, her phoniness. There is more. Her real name, we learn towards the end of the book,

---

4. Capote also got into the "Who Is Holly" sweepstakes, but what he said was almost certainly a deliberate lie, perhaps an attempt to stave off future lawsuits. He traced her lineage to "a German refugee" who arrived in New York City at the age of 17 but—preposterously—spoke English without the trace of an accent.

is "Lulamae," a more than obvious reference to Capote's mother. She's from the South—Texas. And like Lillie Mae's, Holly's parents both died when she was young; she was sent off to live with "different mean people." She and her brother ran away; she wound up marrying a horse doctor at the age of 13. She promised to be his wife and the mother of his many children (whose real mother had died). But she broke their hearts and disappeared—with no cause. She had begun reading the movie star magazines. She got ideas above her station, just like Lillie. And so, with a blind ambition, she transmogrified into Holly Golightly, "glamour girl," "highly publicized girl-about-New York," "Hollywood starlet," famous mainly for being famous; yesterday's Paris Hilton.

Holly is also a drinker, a social climber, a thrower of chaotic parties, and a nutcase prone to violent tantrums—all direct references to Lillie Mae. Even Holly's inadvertent running of messages for the Mob recalls Lillie Mae's equally inadvertent running of Arch's bootleg liquor.

There's a painful episode that occurs more than once during the book. It's a depressing and cruel interlude that gives rise to some violence—or at least fantasies of violence—and its tone makes it stand apart. We discover that Fred is a writer, though unpublished and unknown. He sometimes reads his work to Holly, keen for her approval. The first time she fidgets, frosty-eyed, and moons over her fingernails. Fred's heart contracts. He sees she's utterly uncharmed. "Is that the end?" Holly finally erupts. "Stories about dykes bore the bejesus out of me. I just can't put myself in their shoes."

The next time Holly dissects Fred's work, she seems to be talking about *Other Voices*. "Brats and niggers," she says. "Trembling leaves. Description. It doesn't mean anything. . . . That's how your stories sound. As though you'd written them without knowing the end."

Fred wants to hit her; Holly intuits this. She tells him he'll be sorry. He calls her a prostitute. She lifts herself from a cot, her naked breasts "coldly blue in the sun-lamp light," and tells him to get out.

It's funny how Capote throws this dynamic into the plot. On one hand, at least artistically, he agrees with Holly. *Other Voices* was too precious, too self-consciously literary; so with *Tiffany's* he writes like a reporter, with no fancy, poetical muscle-flexing. But the rejection of his identity as a writer, his principal means of self-definition, this enrages him, almost drives him to violence. Lillie Mae, too, cared little about Truman's genius. She did not want a writer; what she wanted was a man. So Holly is a person Fred loves—he can't help it—but also someone who will not love him or the talents with which he announces himself. As with *Other Voices*, the message becomes: You have only yourself; find a way to separate from those who would disappoint you or misunderstand your giftedness. It is more deactivation: You may wound me in my tenderest spot, but I won't be hurt and I don't need your belief in my ability.

Even when Holly disappears—because, again like Lillie, she refuses to endure the "fade-out" that getting tossed from café society would entail[5]—Fred takes it like a Spartan. You can't really run off and leave everybody, he tells her, but he knows better. Holly has already prepared him, in a speech full of Capote's own hard-won wisdom. "Never love a wild thing. . . . The more you do, the stronger they get. . . . You'll end up looking at the sky. . . . Such an empty place; so vague. Just a country where the thunder goes and things disappear."

It's Lillie Mae in a nutshell: empty, vague, and prone to disappearance.

---

5. This is, funnily enough, a fate Capote would share with Holly when, years later, high society blackballed him for writing *Answered Prayers*.

Capote stuffed a lot of Lillie Mae into "Lulamae" (or Holly); what's even more interesting is that he stuffed a lot of himself into her, too. The overlap is most conspicuous on the psychological side. Holly is told she has a "father-complex" and needs to see a head-shrinker, which she refuses to do. She's a compulsive liar, always telling stories, and until her husband shows up and spills the beans, nobody has the slightest idea where she came from—she's given too many histories, too many times. She suffers from something she calls the "mean reds"—she sweats, she's afraid but can't say of what, she feels a sense of impending doom. It's a textbook anxiety disorder. Capote, too, dealt with constant anxiety, and there were occasions when it was intense. "Something in my life has done a terrible hurt to me," he tells Clarke. "And it seems to be irrevocable." Though he fought the idea when the impetus was his mother's concerns over his sexuality, and though he tended to tell contradictory stories about his mental health history, Capote did consult psychiatrists now and again. Their conclusion? "[Nina] was the cause of all my anxiety— 'free-floating anxiety' is what the psychiatrists say I have. If you've never had it, you don't know what it's like. . . . I live with it constantly. I'm never ever free from it." There's no doubt, Capote said, that the condition stemmed from the hotel room lock-ins, the abandonment and rejection. His subsequent attachment-insecurity led to a baseline psychological state of dread and doom, an ongoing semiconscious notion that harm had him in its sights; he never could say when it might pull the trigger. All he knew for sure was that it would, some day, some way.

Lodging his disorder in Holly helped Capote think through how he might make sense of it. Holly was a mirror. If the character lived with the "mean reds," he could, too; if she did not let it slow her down, neither would he. Fred informs her that what she has is called "angst." And he admits he's had the feeling "quite often." What he recommends is what Capote tried doing: a drink (or two). Holly had taken that path; it didn't help; neither did aspirin or marijuana. (The latter only made her giggle). Holly's best solution wasn't Truman's, but it works for the character (and provides the book's title). She takes a taxi to Tiffany's. The quietness and proud look of the place calm her down immediately. "Nothing very bad could happen to you there," she suggests, "not with those kind men in their nice suits, and that lovely smell of silver and alligator wallets."

Holly also looks like Truman. She's androgynous, boyish, her hair sleek and short as a young man's, with strands of albino-blond and yellow—just like Truman's. She's silly-young, self-amused, and after her arrest she comes across as "not quite 12 years: her pale vanilla hair brushed back." Capote also never looked his age; he played that up, as a way of exaggerating his precocity.

And although Holly was ruthless when it came to Fred's writing, his reason for living, she's the anti-Nina when it comes to sexuality. Capote scripts approval from her; he colors her reassuring. For one thing, she lived with a lesbian and even figures that she may be part "dyke." Everyone is, she says, a little bit gay. "So what?" She also sermonizes in ways Capote couldn't have objected to. "A person ought to be able to marry men or women or—listen, if you [Fred] came to me and said you wanted to hitch up with Man o' War, I'd respect your feeling. No, I'm serious. Love should be allowed. I'm all for it."

Then, because more than anything else Capote feared people who might trick him into thinking they loved him when they didn't, who might hurt him with duplicity, he made Holly, during the same speech, deliver one more Capote-ism: "Good things only happen to you if you're good. . . . Be anything but a coward, a pre-tender, an emotional crook, a whore: I'd rather have cancer than a dishonest heart. . . . Cancer *may* cool you, but the other's sure to."

Trailing infinitely in the wake of Capote's life was a chain of dishonest hearts, from Nina's on; no wonder he ranked such a thing as worse than cancer.

In a number of ways, Holly was a comfort. It's no surprise Capote called her his favorite character. *She was he*, after all, and he was certainly madly in love with himself (with a fervor only the insecure possess). She was Nina, too, but with a couple of refreshing attitudes thrown in antidotally. Her beguilement, then, had several sources, as such things typically do. She blended the two most riveting, consequential, perplexing, and irrepressible currents of Capote's existence: himself and his mother. For these reasons Holly ought to be *sui generis*. But she's not. What attests to her power as an image, an internalized (and externalized) attachment-object, is that she's *not* alone. She may have been the latest and the greatest Capote character, but she had precursors. In his fiction Capote was forever fabricating unstable, bewitching women who put their narrators under their thumb.

"The Headless Hawk," a story Capote worked on along with *Other Voices* (circa 1946, twelve years prior to *Tiffany's*), provides the best example. It's a nightmare tale about a stalker who becomes the prey. It's *Tiffany's* deranged cousin. The main character is going nowhere. He's a poet who's never written poetry, a painter who's never painted, a lover who's never loved, leaving behind a freak's gallery of prior entanglements—stupid Lucille, deaf Connie, and suicidal Gordon. He can only love things that are broken, that show a "broken image of himself."

His name is Vincent, and he works at a gallery—two facts that call van Gogh to mind. One hot July after work, he stands in the street "hunting" passers-by, and presently he sees her: a green-eyed boyish girl in a green raincoat, in dark slacks, a man's white shirt, and huarache sandals. Her eyes have an astonished look, as though they'd witnessed a terrible accident. Her face resembles the faces one sees in paintings of medieval youths. She is 18, just like Holly.

Vincent moves on—puzzlingly, since he started out stalking—but the girl now trails him, trance-eyed, like a sleepwalker, all the way to his home, where she waits on the sidewalk.

Some days later she shows up at the gallery dressed "like a freak" in a lumberjack's shirt and pink ankle socks. She wants to sell a painting she's painted herself, of a headless figure and a headless hawk. Her voice is Southern, and when she unwraps the work, the covering newspaper is the *New Orleans Times-Picayune*—a pair of details pointing in the direction of Lillie Mae.

Vincent keeps running into the girl, who tells him to call her "D.J." Her face is "imposed upon his mind; he could no more dispossess it than could a dead man rid his legendary eyes of the last image seen." D.J. rarely speaks, and when she does, the words make little sense. She isn't even sure what month it is. There's an allusion to her being a former mental patient. She's obsessed with a man named "Mr. Destronelli," whom everybody knows. He "looks like you, like me, like most anybody," she explains. Some nights she thinks she sees him and wanders out to investigate; on one such occasion she threatens a neighbor with a pair of scissors.

Despite her insanity, Vincent admits he loves her. She throws the confession back in his face; his feelings are not returned. At last he tells her she's "crazy," though he does not think that that should make a difference, "a man cannot be held to account for those he loves." Still, in the span of days he comes to fear her, to hide out, his own home a place of dread lest she return to it. A bit like Joel does in *Other Voices*, Vincent catches a fever, pneumonia lasting a long month. His perceptions are hazy. Fantasy and reality intermingle. She won't let him alone. He meets her at his gate, near the gallery, outside restaurants, in thunder under a lamppost, the "wordless pantomime of her pursuit" contracting his heart. She just smiles, madly. It's clear: she will never leave, and Vincent—"a victim, born to be murdered, either by himself or another"—will never be anything more than her possession. A prisoner to a madwoman.

Setting this tale beside *Tiffany's* is instructive. Both feature 18-year-old boyish Southern girls with varying degrees of madness; both feature hapless, besotted, arty "stalkers" in love with wild things that can't be possessed; and both end bitterly. Holly leaves forever, D.J. menaces eternally. "The Headless Hawk" feels a little like a warm-up, *Tiffany's* unconscious. D.J. makes a very, very scary Holly; she's not just zany, she goes after people with sharp objects. Holly (ten years later) is D.J. brightened up. She's still impossible, but at least she's not likely to kill anyone.[6]

This psychotic, unpredictable, unsettling, yet irrepressible female who is both deeply desired and deeply disappointing is Capote's number-one fixation. It's another piece of evidence in support of the "ouch" script already described: expressions of sincere love and need lead to abandonment and betrayal. Vincent spells the formula out clearly in "The Headless Hawk": "good beginnings, always, bad endings, always." Capote's narrators do not *get the girl*; just as Capote did not get Nina. But at the same time, Nina, in real life, wouldn't leave him alone. Drinking more and more, needy in the extreme, throwing tantrums, suicidal, she called Truman day and night, leaning on him for one emotional bailout after another (in ways she never allowed *him* to lean on *her*). As he put it succinctly in a letter from 1963: she "developed mental problems, became an alcoholic, and made my life miserable." There were also unending money needs as Joe's finances tanked; Capote refers at one point to

---

6. Both women share a child doppelganger, the icily merciless towhead Miriam, from the story of the same name, whom I describe in Chapter 5.

the "insolvable Nina and Joe problem." He constantly funneled cash their way, wondering, "How can I keep all that up and be a writer too?"

Somehow he managed. And he did so the same way lots of writers do, by fictionalizing the friction. There's another story, "Shut a Final Door," that Capote especially liked. It's hard to say why, except that it's a perfect summary of his basic dilemma. Walter finds himself in a stifling New Orleans hotel room, just like Truman used to do. He's sick, broken down, afraid to call the bellboy, afraid to leave. The ceiling fan gets him thinking about circles—there is no beginning to its action, no end; everything, he realizes, is a circle.

But all circles have centers, and Walter reflects on what *his* might be—his core, his origin. One thing he's sure of: if there is anything wrong with him, it's beyond his control. It all has a lot to do with hypothetical "Person X." Walter obviously speaks Capote's language: "He needed X's love, but was incapable of loving. He could never be sincere with X, never tell him more than fifty percent of the truth. . . . Somewhere along the line Walter was sure he'd be betrayed. He was afraid of X, terrified." All his life, Walter figures, "some cheat had been dealing him the wrong cards." In fact, "everyday everywhere everyone was being cheated." He was conscious of being unloved, and this knowledge was "like an extra heart beating inside him."

Walter dreams. His father pulls to a curb in a limousine. The door opens. "Daddy," Walter yells, running forward, but the door slams shut, mashing off his fingers; his father only laughs.

"*All our acts are acts of fear*," Walter concludes. A universal psychological law? Unlikely. But a picture of Capote's primary affect style? Definitely. He feared not getting what he wanted: attentive responsiveness. And he feared getting what he wanted: it drove away in black Buicks. What he was left with was love's perfume. He drank it but it wasn't love. And though he had no inkling of this at the time, more fear and loss was in store: much more. Love was about to *literally* die, in the person of a new, unimagined X, Perry Smith. And a succession of mother swans—those featured in *Answered Prayers*—was gassing up different Buicks, set to drive off without the most cursory backward glance. Capote lived life in a checkmate. Whatever move he made, the game was over.

•   •   •

The short stories, *Other Voices*, and *Tiffany's* were the early works published in Capote's lifetime. But there was another ambivalent effort, a novel he never expected to see the light of day. This was *Summer Crossing*, a book of social commentary he labored over in the late 1940s, but finally judged "thin, clever, unfelt." At first it gave him "fine hopes." He felt alive and justified doing it, and it left him nervous all the time, "probably a good sign." By the time he was two-thirds through, some of the book pleased him and some did not, a fact he figured to be natural. He found it turning into something different and "infinitely more complex" than he'd originally intended, so pulling it into shape "will take a monumental effort." The length he guessed would reach 80,000 words in the end—an extreme overestimate, as it turns out, on par with the overestimates Capote later ventured when describing *Answered Prayers*.

So, over a span of several years, the book progressed, though fitfully. Yet in 1953 Capote confessed to Mary Louise Aswell, "It was never finished." He set it aside when *Other Voices* came unbidden and irrepressibly. *Summer Crossing* he "tore up."

Or so he thought. In 2004, Alan Schwartz, Capote's friend, lawyer, and the trustee of his literary properties, got word from Sotheby's that a cache of Capote material had turned up for auction—letters, photographs, and what appeared to be an unpublished novel.

The news was jarring. No one had the vaguest clue what the documents were. Schwartz looked into the matter, and what Sotheby's said (improbably, according to Schwartz in a National Public Radio interview) was this: an "unknown person's" uncle had once house-sat an apartment Capote lived in around 1950, and when Truman vacated, after telling the superintendent to dump his remaining possessions on the street for pickup, this uncle grabbed them, feeling, for some reason, that "he could not let this material be discarded." Capote's biographer, Gerald Clarke, went to look the materials over, and discovered, along with letters, pictures, and annotated manuscripts of some of Capote's early work, a reasonably full draft of the apparently torn up *Summer Crossing*. The book was born again—Capote's very first work, at least before *Other Voices* elbowed it aside. As it happened, not a single soul bid on the materials: first because the price was too high, in Schwartz's view, and second because the Truman Capote Literary Trust retained all publication rights. Eventually, through Schwartz's interventions, the New York Public Library purchased the manuscript, and that is where it resides today—four school notebooks with 62 pages of accompanying notes.

Next came the hardest question: Should a work Capote had judged a failure be published? Schwartz solicited several readings, each essentially favorable, so the decision was made to go ahead. The book appeared in 2005, a short 126-page study of a rich debutante-to-be's summer "home alone" in New York City. As for possible post-hoc tinkerings, according to a note on the text editors corrected only inconsistent usages, misspellings, and punctuation, in a few instances inserting missing words. The "foremost concern" was to "faithfully reproduce the author's manuscript."

As it turns out, despite Capote's misgivings, *Summer Crossing* is a fascinating wedge work—one part *Other Voices*, with language like "doorway megaphones, frenziedly hurling into the glare sad roars of rhythm, accelerate the sense to collapse: run—out of the white into the real, the sexless, the jazzless, the joyful dark," and one part *Tiffany's*. It's not nearly as good as either, but it's also not bad.

"Grady" is the debutante in question, her name arrived at more or less illegitimately—a brother Grady preceded her, stillborn. In her mother's secret opinion, "Grady had never been Grady, not the child she wanted"—she cheated her by "not being born a boy" (Lillie Mae, of course, might have said the same thing of Truman, who was both a boy and not a boy). There's an older sister, Apple, an "assured success," and a father named Lamont; also a close friend, a boy named Peter Bell, usually "perversely dressed" in severe flannel suits or "wild-west belts of jeweled inappropriateness." (Peter recalls Truman's sartorial extravagance back in his Monroeville days).

Mrs. McNeil, Grady's mother, begins the book by telling her, "You are a mystery, my dear"; Grady agrees, and it pleases her to think so. Less pleasantly, her family comes near to thinking Grady "perverse." Her mother, Grady realizes, "loved her without really liking her," while Grady, even as a very small girl, never much liked her mother either. There is only the thinnest contact, no real sympathy; Grady's remoteness suggesting, to her mother, both superiority and contempt. Grady tends to stare through Mrs. McNeil, not at her; the woman is constantly being thrown into battle with "a will-power harder than her own."

The big debut is a bone of contention. Mrs. McNeil's debut was a "famous and sentimental affair," her grandmother, once a celebrated New Orleans beauty, having presented her and her two sisters. Grady doesn't want a dress, and she doesn't want a party. "I will not be made a fool," she intones. It's her parents' habit to wait for her to "act up" like this, inject her "stubborn oddness." But what she feels a good portion of the time is "genuine disinvolvement." Deactivation, in other words.

The action's basic setup is a nifty, fantasized reversal of Capote's own personal trauma: in an abandonment of sorts, the parents leave on an ocean liner to Europe, and Grady *wants* them to go, she is *happy* to be left. Emotionally, she's the one in the driver's seat. And her car is even a big Buick, just like Lillie Mae's, the one Capote watched disappear down dusty Monroeville roads. The parents are very uneasy leaving—at least that's Mrs. McNeil's sentiment. Grady is joyous, set to fly her "pennant high above and in the wind." Freedom is just around the corner.

Though her parents don't know it, what is exciting Grady especially is Clyde, her decidedly lowbrow Jewish paramour. He has friends with names like Mink, Gump, and Bubbles, who clean their nails with pocket knives, smoke reefer, and speak with "mumbling power," always hoarse and furry, fond of the double-negative. In their very first exchange, Clyde tells Grady not to "nigger lip" a cigarette.

Clyde is on a road to nowhere. He lives at home with his mother and siblings, father absent and unmentioned. There was a stint in the army, a short-lived venture with an uncle who owns a luggage company, whose sluttish daughter made Clyde the prime target of her affections. For a time he dreamed of being a ballplayer; he was a sandlot standout, a talented pitcher. But no offers came, so he settled for work as a garage attendant, sleeping the day away in strangers' cars. Grady's dreams are Clyde-cluttered. In them she's "perpetually the spectator," Clyde with someone else, some other girl, with whom he walks past, "smirking disdainfully or dismissing [Grady] by look-ing the other way." In fact, in reality, too, Grady is chronically alarmed by the "meagerness" of Clyde's inquiries, his basic indiffer-ence, the prospect that he might dissolve. She fantasizes reaching him somehow, and "as a leaf folds before wind or a flower bends beneath the leopard's foot," submitting to his "lunging, loin-deep" powers.

"Say you love me," she pleads. "I said it," he replies. "No, oh no. You haven't. I was listening. And you never do." Though the words don't come, he tattoos her name on his body—G-R-A-D-Y.

After a loud, hot, hallucinatory night in the city, its nerves sizzling "like the wires inside a lightbulb," the two impulsively marry in Red Bank, New Jersey, despite the fact that Grady is only seventeen. Later Grady learns she's pregnant after a romp in her family's Fifth Avenue apartment. From here, as in *Other Voices*, the narrative grows internally preoccupied, and reality recedes. The pace also picks up, as if Capote knows he needs to corral all the plot and character elements and get to some kind of finish line. On the heels of a vaguely described fight with Clyde's family during which Clyde apparently strikes his adored mother, Grady careers off to the Hamptons and her sister Apple's home, where clocks wink maliciously, each registering different hours, and the heat closes in like a hand over a murder victim's mouth. She sits for hours naked on the beach, talking to herself. She realizes, "If I die, all this will go on." The probably gay Peter shows up to tell her she's in "a bad way," but then promptly leaves. Next Clyde tracks her down, with his friend Gump. They motor to a bar in the city where they all get high, Grady included. Peter materializes, intent on snatching Grady away, saving her from herself, but Clyde smashes him. Staring silently, like a bird stunning itself by "dashing against walls and glass," Grady grabs the car steering wheel as it skids across the Queensboro Bridge. "Damn it, you'll kill us," Gump screams. "I know," says Grady. No one gets out alive. The book ends with a kind of murder-suicide.

Capote said *Summer Crossing* lacked the qualities of a "personal vision," the "anxieties" crowding his other early works. I'm not so sure. It's certainly slight, a hackneyed, rich-girl-meets-poor-bad-boy potboiler, but it's got the Capote stamp—moments of gorgeous prose, and all the trademark themes. Wild spirit Grady, indomitable like Truman, flicks aside her mother's entreaties, blows off her sister Apple, and simultaneously finds and loses herself (with collateral damage). Can one really leave behind family and a clueless, self-involved mother? Maybe, but it sure ain't easy. One can stay, and go slowly mad. Or one can try taking off, and dying. It's the same Capote Catch-22: how to go it alone without going crazy. Grady craves the warm, almost "erotic" atmosphere of filial togetherness, but like Capote's, her "system required the cold, exclusive climate of the individual." Pressures of intimacy would only wither her. She's got Truman's mix of attachment strategies: desperately searching for love, fearful of losing it, but running when things begin to look the least bit shaky.

Other conflicts playing themselves out in the book include homosexuality and its doomed transgressiveness. Grady's not sup-posed to love oily losers like Clyde. That's not who she's meant to be; it's unnatural, it's a slap in her family's face. Once Grady kissed a girl, scholarly, bourgeois Naomi, who wrote her passionate poems that really rhymed. But there was no love; Grady had "liked too much to be alone." Besides, it's very seldom that a person loves anyone "they cannot in some way envy"—and Naomi was not enviable, so Grady lost her on purpose, "like an old letter." Peter's the most hapless figure of all. Clyde calls him a fairy and beats him silly. Peter thinks he might love Grady, he thinks they might end up together, but it's also "possible that he never *could* make love with her"; passion between them would be "ludicrous," and so, in moments, he despises her. He wants to want her, but it makes no sense. His waywardness puts him in the car that night, and he dies with the rest of them. In fact, it's as if he died *because* he never avowed his true nature; he'd be alive if he had given up the pretense of heterosexuality. His repression kills him.

And Grady? One reviewer dismissed her as "Holly Golightly Lite." It's true—with the discovery of the *Summer Crossing* manuscript, she becomes the new first in a farrago of doppelgangers, the consistency in the details astonishing. Grady is yet another "tomboy" with "chopped hair"; like D.J.'s, her eyes are "green" and "estimating." People around her sense she's "a girl to whom something was going to happen." She's a "crazy kid," a "mystery," and no one understands her. She's beset by a "nervous wild vigor," mean reds demanding steeper feats, "more daring exertions." She can't help driving too fast, because the speed numbs her, turns out the lights in her mind, deadens "the excess of feeling that made personal contacts so painful." If others strike the keys too hard, she plays them back "too loud." She's full of risk, full of adventure, but she never knows how far she'll go or where it's going to take her. Holly hooks up with Sally Tomato, and the deal goes bad; Grady hooks up with Clyde and his pals, and that deal goes bad, too.

Capote can't seem to stop making the same girl up, manufacturing the same beguiling, yet unreachable, androgynous demon. His situation mirrors Peter Bell's. He loves the girl, he really does. But he envies her more, he wants to be her. At one point Peter realizes that what Grady did, maybe more than anything else, was help him "to pass as a man." Few know he's more her than he is himself; after all, her elegance and her judgments of taste result from "his own tutoring." She's his creation, for which he pays a price. The creation does him in.

Like Peter, Capote's in the car, but it's the girl who grabs the steering wheel.

4 | THE MIND OF A MURDERER

It is a mystery what yoked Capote to *In Cold Blood*, his "nonfiction novel" about the murder of the Clutters, a farm family in Kansas. Nothing he had done cleared the way for this particular development. *Breakfast at Tiffany's* was quite a bit more than a stone's throw from Holcomb, the scene of the murders. Gone were the perplexingly enchanting tomboyish females, replaced by a pair of killers. Gone (for the most part) was the aberrant sexuality. Gone was the quirky Southern gothicism, the fantasy, the strangeness, the immersion in a psychological unreality. Capote now entered the realm of the super-real, of straightforward reportage. It was a task he was just barely up to. He loved it; he hated it. Literally, it almost killed him. Psychologically, it left him on the threshold of madness. Artistically, he intuited, in pretty short order, that what he had on his hands was a masterpiece. But could he bring it off?

The story goes that Capote got the idea for the book out of the blue, after coming across a one-column item about the murders on page thirty-nine of *The New York Times* ("Prominent wheat grower slain"). This was in mid-November of 1959, a year after the appearance of *Breakfast at Tiffany's*. Others dispute this. Brendan

Gill, for instance, who worked at *The New Yorker* for sixty years, said, "Wallace Shawn [*The New Yorker's* editor] told Truman he was interested in seeing the effect of a murder." Slim Keith, one of a legion of Capote's close female friends he called his "swans," remembered Capote's being given a choice of assignments: he could follow a "day lady" around New York and write portraits of the people she worked for, or he could trudge off to Kansas where a heinous, random murder had occurred. Keith's suggestion? "Do the easy one; go to Kansas."

It was not "easy." But Kansas won out.

Capote's initial intention, short-lived, was to write a relatively modest piece, with *The New Yorker* bankrolling an investigative excursion. Capote would focus—just as Shawn had suggested he do—on the echoes of the murders within the tiny Holcomb community. But like many modest plans sometimes do, this one exploded. Capote was locked into a work that had no boundaries, and whose time frame was beyond his control. This was real life, and real life is messy, undefined. Write away as he may, the book was held hostage by the facts of the case. The case needed to reach its conclusion before Capote could formulate his. And for someone so used to imposing imagination on the world at his will, ordering and controlling the facts he chose to manipulate, *In Cold Blood* represented an altogether different kind of challenge. He almost couldn't take it. He was powerless.

But in the beginning he went at the research tenaciously. It was, by all accounts, a sight to behold. At first Capote did not feel particularly safe. The murderers remained at large when he headed out west, and the crime was believed to be local. Friends worried Capote might become a target, especially with all the nosing around he was planning to do. So he took with him Harper Lee, author of *To Kill*

a Mockingbird, a tough woman with a gift for appeasing the locals.[1]
They all adored her, and found her to be an "absolutely fantastic
lady." They did not adore Capote, at least not at first. He had a way
of rubbing the various lawyers, detectives, and KBI (Kansas Bureau
of Investigation) agents the wrong way. After a time, wising up, perhaps, he bought a pair of boots and a cowboy hat. But when Capote
arrived around Thanksgiving, his attire consisted of a small cap, a
sheepskin coat, a long, narrow scarf that trailed to the ground, and a
pair of moccasins. He made no concession to local color, in other
words. On one occasion, Capote met up with a group of KBI agents
in his room after dinner. He paced the floor in a new pink negligée,
telling them all about the book he planned. As Agent Nye later
put it: "I did not get a very good impression of the little son of a
bitch. . . and that impression never changed."

Fortunately for Capote, not everyone was left with the same
enduring frou-frou image. Slowly but surely, drawing on the people
skills his insecure attachment history required—that sixth sense for
pulling out of people what he needed—Capote managed to win
over key players, most notably Alvin Dewey, the agent in charge of
the investigation. He also got close to Dewey's wife, Marie, and their
son, who was interested in writing. Over many months Capote read
the young Dewey's nascent fiction efforts, advising him on books to
read and matters of style. Capote owed the Deweys, and he knew it.
Without their help, the book would not have come off. Their assis-
tance was absolutely critical.

Neither Capote nor Lee took notes. Their habit was to conduct
interviews, separately sequester themselves in their rooms, write
or type out what they remembered, then compare notes. It was

---

1. Lee, too, had an interest in reportage. She told Capote about wanting to do some sort
of investigative piece on the Ku Klux Klan.

labor-intensive. It produced thousands of pages of material, much of which never made it into the finished product. Capote also purchased the transcript of record, the court proceedings, and "if you had that," according to Dewey, "you had the whole story."

Though Capote liked to insist on the scrupulous factualness of what he wrote, the reality was more complicated. After all, to this point he was a fantasist, his mode in *Other Voices* and in many of the early stories. His imagination took him places even he could not foresee. He gave it free rein; he turned it loose. The discipline of reportage was a mindset to which he was temperamentally unsuited. In one instance, Nye refused to approve galleys. He felt Capote fictionalized people to a degree that was "way out of character." "It was just not written truthfully," Nye said. "I was under the impression that the book was going to be factual, and it was not; it was a fiction book." Nye relented, but only after a lot of back and forth (and in the end, he found the book "tremendous," un-put-downable).

This insistence on his faithfulness to fact and on how the book's every word was grounded in material assiduously collected through either interviews or transcript-procurement was incredibly important to Capote stylistically. I said that Capote's attraction to the subject was a mystery. It is, in large part. It came out of nowhere. But *some* of the appeal—and this turns out to be true in the case of *Answered Prayers*, as well—revolved around a literary theory he had harbored ever since he began writing professionally: "It seemed to me that journalism, reportage, could be forced to yield a serious new art form: the 'nonfiction novel,' as I thought of it." And for Capote, narrative reporting *did* leave room for the imagination, broadly defined. Facts were not imagined—he was adamant about that—but they needed to be imaginatively arranged, ordered, unfolded; one had to become a "literary photographer" with a 20/20 eye for visual detail, albeit an "exceedingly selective one." Above all, he had to empathize "with personalities outside his usual imaginative range, mentalities unlike his own, kinds of people he would never have written about had he not been forced to by encountering them inside the journalistic situation." So Capote was pushing himself and his art into virgin territory. He was not grabbed immediately by the *material*—though in time he researched murder and murderers and developed his own ideas about the psychology of killers. What *really* attracted him was the possibility of a new form, a new mode of expression that liberated all the powers at his disposal. Capote was a born stylist; it was in his blood, his DNA. He mastered style as an adolescent, by writing to the point where craft became second nature. *In Cold Blood* was another effort to refine and expand his powers, to test what he was capable of. It was an exercise Capote took deadly seriously.

And in reading through Capote's letters between 1959 and 1965, when the book was finally completed, two things quickly become obvious: the stakes and the strain. In no time at all, Capote was swept away. He forced himself to live quietly, in various rented locations throughout Europe, where he wrote most of the manuscript. He saw almost no one. And he was totally concentrated on the book, which, he told his editor, Bennett Cerf, "is going to be a masterpiece: I mean that. Because if it isn't, then it's nothing." One month later he informed Newton Arvin, "It has to be perfect. . . . Sometimes when I think how good it *could* be, I can hardly breathe." That whip Capote kept for self-flagellation was working overtime. He had a habit of ratcheting up expectations—he later did the same in the case of *Answered Prayers*, with far more disastrous results. Announcing to everyone involved that, this time, it was all-or-nothing, perfection or failure, virtually required a creative frenzy. He was setting the bar high, and he was inviting others to impose the same standard. In a way, it was a move that externalized his motivation, already internally secure (on most days, at least).

Maybe unsurprisingly, in light of all the masterpiece talk, the work was incredibly tough going. Capote's emotions were all over the place. One day he was ecstatic; the next, morose. He reported feeling "very excited," "totally dedicated," "emotionally involved in a sense that I have seldom been before." Worried about sounding more than a little pretentious, he noted a sense of "great obligation" to the material and the people in the book; to some degree he was writing for them, the book an act of empathy, an act of love. Capote worried over the work day and night, it never left his mind, it never left him alone; it became, almost from day one, a "monumental obsession." The chaos of the information he had in hand was a colossal strain to craft; he compared the job to "doing the finest needlework."

This exuberance, the sense of nobility of purpose and of grandeur of theme, was less common than its opposite, though. For one thing, Capote had never worked so hard. Compared to *In Cold Blood*, his earlier writing had come easily. It was effortlessly controlled. It was stylistically familiar. It came directly *out of his head*— no notes, no interviews, no real people to capture. It was not a grind, it was unfettered imagination. Now the emotion most conspicuously present was dread. "It is so painful," Capote said, that "I don't know that I can live with it that long without having a crack-up." He felt more and more limp and numb and "horrified." He had awful dreams "every night." He was depressed; again and again he wondered if he could endure mentally—"this sort of sustained creative work keeps one in a constant state of tension." The strain was too much. Every morning, Capote said, after nights of miserable dreams, he threw up.

It was not so much *thinking* about the book that was a problem; Capote enjoyed his obsession. He scarcely thought of anything else.

He went into what he called "trance-like states" that lasted three or four hours. The odd part was, he hated to *work* on it, to actually *write*. It exhausted him, left him "tense as nine newly tuned pianos." Despite his intentions, his devotion to narrative nonfiction, the form came to repulse him. It annoyed and frustrated him. Even early on in the process, in late 1960, he declared: "This is my last attempt at reportage. . . . If I manage to bring this off, I will have said all I have to say about the particular technique. . . . God, I wish it were over." What he did not know was that he had five onerous years to go. It was not even close to being "over." The book had "imprisoned" him. He compared it to an illness—he could not bear to be away from it, nor could he bear to be with it. He woke with "a feeling of awful sadness." He tried concentrating on "Something Else"—it was pointless. He could not. "Nothing could ever compensate me," he concluded, "for the amount of work and suffering that has gone into this book." His entire future as an artist was at stake, he realized, and on top of the work itself, the thought "just *undoes* me."

And it only got worse. In early 1961, his beloved bulldog Bunky died—he had had the dog eight years, and loved him more than anything in the world. For Capote, it was like losing a child. Then, after 20 years of chain-smoking Chesterfields, he was forced to give the habit up, on doctor's orders. He developed angina spasms, caused, it was believed, by nicotine poisoning. The pain was "sort of like having an endless series of little heart attacks." Later, still in continuous pain, his symptoms received a new diagnosis: a crushed spinal nerve. The work suffered; his infirmities distracted him mightily. He noted that he was drinking martinis by the gallon; his doctor even called them an "antidote." In the summer of 1962, Capote reported a severe attack of rheumatism in his writing wrist. Pills chased it away "for the moment." Out of nowhere, in May, 1964, he cited "trouble" with his upper lip. Cancer was suspected. He was not certain, at first, what sort of treatment might be required. But the biopsy came back negative: "and though there is something wrong it ain't cancer!" Finally, while on the verge of finishing the book's final pages, Capote succumbed to Asian flu. There was some consolation, though. After reading a sizeable portion of the *In Cold Blood* manuscript, the *New Yorker's* Wallace Shawn cabled: "Incomparable. An authentic masterpiece."

His body racked, his dog dead, his nerves shot, his sanity in serious question, barely giving "a fuck anymore *what* happens," Capote, by some providential miracle, had reached a finish line. "Bless Jesus," he exclaimed. "Incredible to suddenly be free. . . . Never again!" The book, he called the most interesting experience of his life. It was fearsome, it was brutal, it was a torturous master. It owned him for six years. It was the artistic equivalent of Nina— one long soul-sapping harangue. It changed his life; altered his point of view "about almost everything."

The art reached an end. He had invented, he felt, a new style. But there were sinister aftershocks. As his friend, John Knowles, explained, "He lost a grip on himself after that. . . . That's when he began to unravel." And though he had come close to a breakdown at several points during the writing process, those body-blows were nothing compared to what was in fact the most painful aspect of the entire experience: the trauma of the executions. Because, as he wrote away, as he disappeared into Europe, isolating himself on behalf of the work, he grew closer and closer, emotionally, to the killers. He even kept up a running correspondence with them. One of the killers, Richard Hickock, was a "full-time nobody," according to his wife; the same could not be said of accomplice Perry Smith. With Smith, Capote ran full-tilt into a second self, an alternate life he might have lived *if not for* X, Y, and Z. And in a way, a twisted, hopeless, irrational, and very destructive way, Capote was mesmerized.

Murder and murderers had never before crossed Capote's mind. "Up to that particular time I wasn't interested in crime and didn't know anything about it." He was mulling over several possible writing projects, but "certainly crime was not one of them." Capote did not select the Clutter murders, he did not select *In Cold Blood*—"it selected *me*." And from that moment on, it was full-speed ahead.

Capote turned himself into a crime expert, a specialist on the killing mind. He read true-crime accounts, pored over murder encyclopedias. He did his homework, in other words. Once the autodidact, always the autodidact. There was primary research, too. He estimated he personally interviewed more than 30 killers, in the process developing different mini-theories of homicidal behavior, some chiefly descriptive. Murderers were tattooed, he noticed. This was one uniformity[2]. They also laughed eerily while detailing crimes; another interesting puzzle. But more psychologically, according to Capote, "all had experienced a childhood marked by parental brutality, rejection, insecurity"—that was the conclusion of a team of psychiatrists from the Menninger Clinic in an article titled "Murder Without Apparent Motive." "The arbitrary act of violence," Capote came to believe, "springs from the poverty of a life [steeped in] deep insecurity and emptiness." Additional common characteristics uncovered by the Menninger researchers include the blurring of boundaries between fantasy and reality, periods of altered states of consciousness (trancelike states), blunted emotional reactions, and a primitive fantasy life.

---

2. Smith and Hickock conformed to this rule. Smith's tattoos included the name of a nurse, Cookie, who had tended to him after an accident, along with an orange-eyed, red-fanged tiger, a spitting snake coiled around a dagger, a pile of skulls, a tombstone, and a chrysanthemum. Hickock wore a blue dot under his eye—signifying that he'd been in prison—a blue grinning cat face, a blue rose, the head of a dragon, a gremlin with a pitchfork, even the word "peace" accompanied by a cross radiating rays of holy light.

Parental rejection, deep insecurity, trancelike states, fantasy-proneness, suppressed emotion: the list sounds familiar. It may describe some murderers. It certainly describes Capote. There is small chance that this unnerving convergence was lost on him. It must have tossed him sideways. *He had the mind of a murderer.*[3] Getting to know killers was, therefore, simultaneously, getting to know shards of himself, his own haunted history, his basic tendencies. And the process came to pivot around Perry Smith, Capote's evil twin.

Hickock was of the garrulous tradition. He was the one Capote got to know first; Smith was initially guarded, cornered, paranoid. Once Hickock started talking—and it did not take much—he couldn't stop. And he talked to anyone, anywhere. He had a virtually photographic memory, and Capote plied him for details. He laid out the killers' peripatetic odyssey down to its last bathetic vibration. Though Hickock was a nonstop blabber, he never spoke to Capote's condition. There was no deep affinity. He had what Capote termed a "check-bouncing mentality"—the sly, quick mind of a petty thief. He didn't want to kill; he was reluctant. He wanted to be a big shot, wanted to throw his weight around, according to KBI agent Dewey, but he wasn't the deadly type. Still, Hickock recognized Perry's deadliness and attached himself to it and encouraged it, though he found Smith "scary as hell"; he also arranged

---

3. "Everyone at one time or another has wanted to kill someone," Capote once said. "The true reason why many people commit suicide is because they are cowards who prefer to murder themselves rather than murder their tormentor. As for me, if desire had ever been transferred into action, I'd be right up there with Jack the Ripper." Capote also told the story of his doctor's suggesting that he find a healthy hobby. Can you think of anything? the doctor asked. "Yes, murder," said Capote. "He laughed, we both did, except I wasn't laughing." On yet another occasion, Capote told a friend: "Some people kill with swords and some people kill with words."

the crime. In a sense, though it's a bit of an overstatement, Hickock was the brains behind the operation. An IQ test performed in prison showed his to be around 130, roughly 30 to 40 points above the average inmate's. He'd heard from a fellow prisoner who once worked for the Clutters about a safe in the house with large amounts of cash. The crime was a cinch, an easy score. They'd grab the dough, then hightail it for Mexico.

In fact there was no money. Little matter: Hickock always had alternate designs, anyway. Ever since hearing about the Clutters, he had fixated on young Nancy, sight unseen. He fantasized about raping her. So, with the money crossed out of the equation, rape became Hickock's agenda. Smith being, according to Capote, a "little moralist"—though, at the same time, paradoxically lacking the conscience he wished he'd had—the rape idea enraged Perry. He pressed Hickock to kill the Clutters, but Hickock wasn't up to it. For all his tough talk about "splattering the walls with hair," Hickock could *plan* murder but not *commit* it. At this point, now inside the Clutter home, Smith had, in Capote's words, a "brain explosion." He strode to the basement, where Mr. Clutter was tied up, and shoved a knife through his throat. Then he shot him in the head. Next, according to most investigators, Smith killed the rest of the family—Clutter's wife Bonnie; Kenyon, 15; and Nancy, 16.

To the end, and even to this day, there is some dispute about who did what. Hickock contended that Smith committed all four killings. Capote felt the same way. KBI agent Dewey believed Hickock and Smith each killed two family members. Early on, in fact, Dewey took Smith's detailed statement. He said he had killed Mr. Clutter and his son, and that Hickock took care of the women. Then, just as the statement was being typed up for him to sign, Smith recanted. He requested a change. He said, "I was talking to Hickock and he doesn't want to die with his mother thinking he'd committed two of those murders. I have no folks, they don't care about me or anything, so why don't we just make it [that I killed all four]." Dewey believed Smith's first declaration. Capote, as I said, believed the second one.

At any rate, Hickock and Smith agreed that killing someone was easier than cashing a bad check. And it didn't need to make any sense at all; it required no special motive. "I didn't want to harm the man," Smith later explained. "I thought he was a very nice gentleman. I thought so right up to the moment I cut his throat." The Clutters had, of course, never done anything to Smith. But as he figured it, they were the ones who needed to pay nonetheless. If he had the semblance of a theory for his own actions that night, it revolved around simple *displacement*. He took his rage out on the Clutters. This was, in its simplest terms, Capote's explanation, as well: "The why is quite clear. Perry identified Mr. Clutter, an authority figure, with the father he loved-hated and he unleashed all his inner resentment in an act of violence. . . . The person Perry was murdering that night in a Kansas farmhouse was not Mr. Clutter but his own father." To the list of killer characteristics Capote shared we can now add another: father love-hate.

But what was the *source* of Smith's rage? An incredibly over-determined one, as usual. He was born in 1928 in Nevada. His parents worked the rodeo circuit, performing as "Tex and Flo." John, his father, was a redheaded Irishman, and his mother, Florence, a full-blooded Cherokee. In 1929 the family—Smith had three siblings, Fern, Barbara, and Jimmy—moved to Alaska, where John bootlegged whiskey (one of Arch's avocations too). John was abusive; Flo drank and philandered. Money always tight, the family lived on condensed milk and Hershey's Kisses for days at a time, according to Capote. In 1935, Tex and Flo split up. Flo took the kids to San Francisco, where her drinking continued unabated. She died when Smith was thirteen, and he and his siblings were placed in a Catholic orphanage. A wild child and a bed-wetter with "weak kidneys," Smith came in for (alleged) abuse at the hands of the nuns and caseworkers. He was beaten with a black belt, for starters. A creatively sadistic cottage mistress in a detention home—a woman later discharged—was said to have placed some sort of burning ointment on his penis, a torture that apparently amused her ("she thought it was very funny"). Then, in a later orphanage, a caretaker tried drowning him—holding Perry in tubs of ice water until he was blue in the face. At adolescence, Smith reunited with his father but also spent time in different "juvy" facilities for petty crime. He joined a street gang.

There were dreams or fantasies, as there would be, of miraculous escape, or revenge of a ghastly variety. One of these sounded suspiciously Joel Knoxian, recalling the swamps patrolled by Jesus Fever in *Other Voices*. It was a dream of Perry's that recurred. In it he finds himself in Africa (where Holly disappeared), alone, moving through jungle trees. Blue leaves and diamonds hang everywhere—"diamonds like oranges." Perry wants to pick a bushel, but he knows if he does, "a snake is gonna fall on me," a fat "son of a bitch" living in the branches, jealously guarding the jewels. He decides to take his chances. He says he wants the diamonds more than he fears the snake. So he reaches up and yanks at one, but the snake lands on top of him. The two wrestle around, but the serpent's a "slippery sonofabitch." Perry hears his own legs cracking; the snake is swallowing him, feet first. He's being eaten alive. Just then a "hovering avenger," a yellow parrot, "taller than Jesus," comes to his aid, devours the snake, and wings him away to paradise.

This parrot's service varied. It came to Smith's fantasized aid as necessary. He recalled a nun beating him with a flashlight until it broke, after which she "went on hitting me in the dark." Again the "warrior-angel" materialized, blinding the nun with its beak, feeding on her eyes, slaughtering her as she pleaded for mercy. Later the parrot took out, in turn, older children, Smith's father, faithless girls, and a sergeant he'd known in the army. Dick heard this tale recounted at the same time as did Truman. "I'm a normal," Dick interjected. "I only dream about blond chicken."

During the trial's *voir dire* proceedings, Smith (and Hickock, too) composed an autobiography at the request of a psychiatrist, Dr. Jones, who had examined him. Father issues surfaced inevitably. "I loved my father," Smith figured, "but there were times when this love and affection I had for him drained from my heart like wasted water, whenever he would not try to understand my problems, give me a little consideration & voice & responsibility." Feeling, wisely, that he had to get away, at sixteen Smith joined the merchant marine, then the army—the recruiting office gave him a break and "upped" his test, fabricating a higher score than he had actually earned. That led, not to appreciation, but "hatred and bitterness." The last thing Smith ever wanted was charity. There were regular violent outbursts. Smith threw a Japanese policeman off a bridge, he demolished a Japanese café, he stole a Japanese taxicab. Two courts-martial resulted, and Smith was sent back to the States, where he finished out his service at Fort Lewis, Washington.

Two of Smith's siblings committed suicide, including a brother who had been the head of his class. As Capote declares, "That shows how really awry the background of the Smiths' lives were."

It's an awryness Hickock's early life surprisingly lacked. His parents were farm workers. His school years "went quite the same as most other boys my own age." There were fights, girls, new bicycles to ride. Hickock was "hardly ever allowed" to leave his yard, however. His father was strict "in that line." He recalled just one argument his mother and father had had, about what, exactly, he couldn't say. The house was always neat, the family had "clean clothes aplenty." Dick was a popular student-athlete in high school, receiving nine letters in all—basketball, football, track, baseball—before head injuries from a motorcycle accident threw him seriously off-stride, also disfiguring his face. When his eyes looked straight ahead, his face looked to the right.

Some, like Marie Dewey, Alvin Dewey's wife, claim Capote disliked Hickock. That's true—at least in relative terms. The far more elusive, more complex, deadlier Smith was Capote's number-one obsession. But in sifting through Capote's reflections on the pair, one finds that he was unexpectedly impartial—to a point. Hickock and Smith he called "very very good friends of mine, perhaps the closest friends I've ever had in my life, very very close intimates in every conceivable way." *In every conceivable way*? A puzzling prepositional phrase, to say the least (and one we return to later).

Smith was Capote's fork in the road. Their lives had led them along a similar path. Capote turned right, Perry left. There's a contact sheet of Capote and Smith produced by Richard Avedon (who also shot Smith and Hickock alone).[4] They stand side by side. In most images, Capote seems to be interrogating Perry, who wears a white shirt and jeans. Capote is in a suit and glasses, with a bow tie. They look to be approximately the same height, Smith perhaps an inch taller. Physically, they were a close match. They shared the same smallness, a pixielike, elfin appearance. But Smith was dark—black hair, black eyebrows, brownish skin from his mother's Cherokee

---

4. The "alone" shots feature the pair's tattoos: they lift their shirt sleeves to reveal them. Hickock's face is clearly pressed sideways (the motorcycle accident). His expression is cold, faintly angry. Smith comes across as a lovable loser, his look quite a bit more welcoming.

side. Capote, still quite slender at the time, was pale, his hair dirty-blond.

Then there were the life-history similarities, too: Alcoholic mothers, fathers mainly out of the picture, childhood rejection and insecurity, getting fobbed off on others to raise (Capote had aunts; Perry, nuns), suicide (Capote's mother, Smith's siblings). Capote never professed much hope for Hickock, but he opposed capital punishment, and always maintained that Smith, at least, could have been rehabilitated. Just like Capote, Smith from a very early age consoled himself with art. He wanted to paint and write. He was a gifted musician with a natural ear, playing five or six instruments, the guitar his favorite. But what he told Capote again and again—a remark that no doubt hit home—was that never in his life had anyone, not his father nor the different reform-school staff members, "encouraged him in any single creative thing he wanted to do." He tried to make someone interested in him, but nobody ever paid the slightest attention. As a result, Capote theorized, he lived in a "schizophrenic dream fantasy"—a defense against the total absence of sustained affection. His bitter feeling of being deprived and alone, "ousted from the world," simply festered. Lacking guidance of any kind, lacking love, he found no effective outlet. But to the last, he never stopped trying. On death row he avidly read the books Capote sent ("I put him on a systematic reading program"), growing particularly enamored of Thoreau and Santayana, writing Capote long letters in which he dissected and analyzed their ideas.

Capote reciprocated; he wrote both Smith and Hickock twice per week. Once, to Smith, he felt a need, after waking in the middle of the night, to briefly lay out his life history—"which has a few certain similarities to yours." It was a mainly factual account, with one or two exaggerations (he said his parents divorced when he was three, not seven). He noted his intellectual and artistic precocity and his emotional immaturity, and then allowed, "I always had emotional problems—largely because of a 'question' you yourself asked me on our last visit and which I answered truthfully." The question Smith asked was whether Capote was gay.

Homosexuality in fact hovered constantly on the fringe of the Capote–Smith relationship. To some, as we will see, it was not just on the fringe but at the dead center of everything tying the two together. An extraverted bad-boy athlete, Hickock was the classic ladies' man, an accomplished tail-chaser. Smith, not so much. Capote's interest was obviously piqued. In interviews he came across as more than fractionally preoccupied with the matter of Perry's sexual orientation. And in some ways, Capote's conclusions were all over the map. He said, for instance, that Perry was essentially *asexual*. When virile Dick frequented whorehouses in Mexico, Smith sat in cafés, waiting. He wanted none of it. He found it repellent, dirty. Only once did the pattern vary: an old queen ushered out a female midget, leaving the similarly dwarfish Smith "madly excited." To Capote, this was an exception that proved the rule.

On the other hand, Smith's love for another con, Willie-Jay, was profound, Capote insisted—"but never consummated physically, though there was the opportunity," as there always is in prison. (Sex is incredibly easy to come by behind bars, and it does not require any special cleverness.) Perry had at least one homosexual affair, Capote revealed, and "definite homosexual fixations," too. There was a *non sequitur* moment in an interview Capote gave in 1968 in which, out of the blue, Capote declared there was no homosexual relationship between Hickock and Smith. How could he be so sure? Because "they were completely frank about such matters and would have told me like a shot."

It is hard to say how good Capote's word is here. It's true that Hickock and Smith trusted him, told him things they kept from others. But *everything*? Maybe, maybe not. Hickock especially would have drawn scant pleasure from confessions of inversion, being a boastful man's man, an aggressive heterosexual. Plus, Capote figured Smith both ways—he was sexless but homosexually fixated. He was a sermonizing psychopath. Just like Freud in his analysis of Leonardo da Vinci—a book largely doomed by the master's projections of his own acknowledged homosexual feelings—Capote was determined to make Perry gay, but only *passively* so. He had his tendencies, but he rarely acted on them. He was a fragile innocent. He was a bit of a virgin, all things being equal.

A minority contingent of *In Cold Blood* figures and analysts chose *not* to take Capote at his word. A handful of interesting ideas have been raised by critics—all conjectural, but not without merit. As a preliminary matter, there is disagreement about the degree of Capote's direct access to Smith. Charles McAtee, former Kansas Director of Penal Institutions—a man, therefore, very much in the know—claims Capote only visited the killers twice before their execution. He *corresponded* with them—"over our objections"—but the author and killers rarely sat face to face. McAtee explains: "Warden Crouse knew that Truman was homosexual and he thought the last thing in the world that he needed was to put up with a known homosexual visiting two guys on death row. He has enough problems with homosexuality inside the prison."

Others suggest Capote had *carte blanche*, having bribed a high-ranking official with a $10,000 note (this was, in fact, Capote's contention). The question turns out to be important, for this reason. KBI agent Nye—the man who saw more fiction in *In Cold Blood* than fact—created a serious stir in 1997 by claiming that Capote and Smith were lovers. It's a notion pushed explicitly in both recent Hollywood versions of the *In Cold Blood* saga, *Capote* and *Notorious*. "I can't prove it," Nye admits, "but they spent a lot of time up there in the cell, [Capote] spent a considerable amount of money bribing the guard to go around the corner, and they were both homosexuals and that was what happened, I wasn't there, so. . . ."

Nye never developed his hunch any further. He just tossed it out there as grist for the mill. And it depends entirely, of course, on *access*—of a rather extensive kind. McAtee denies such access existed; Nye assumes that it did. In any case, Nye made his suggestion, one he had no interest in furthering.

But ex-convict, crime-writer J. J. Maloney, did. It's a unique perspective. Maloney had a bit of Perry Smith in him. He spent several years in reform schools, and 13 years in prison for murder and armed robbery. He used the jail time well, becoming an artist, poet, and book reviewer for the *Kansas City Star*. Later he founded *Crime Magazine*—an "encyclopedia of crime from prisons and parole to serial killers and assassinations." Somewhere along the line he developed a particular fascination with *In Cold Blood*, the true motive for the murders, and the subject of Capote's honesty.

First off, Maloney felt Capote romantically idealized Smith while turning Hickock into a monster, the kind of man who swerves his car for the pleasure of running over stray dogs, a pedophile with "several sample experiences" under his chronically loosened belt. To Maloney, the portrayals were laughably tendentious. Smith wasn't really some sort of unintentional, misunderstood killer whose brain exploded, and Hickock wasn't pure irredeemable evil. The truth was far less bifurcated.

Maloney also contended that, contrary to Capote's position, Smith and Hickock *were* lovers. Having seen, firsthand, the dynamics of prison sexuality at work, Maloney figured Smith for a "punk"— a small, weak, passive con who satisfies the sexual needs of one tougher, more masculine. Such homosexual behavior is situational.

It need not continue outside of the joint. In fact, it typically doesn't. The sex inside is a matter of expedience, of need.

Three things led Maloney to this conclusion: Smith's enraged response on finding Hickock in Nancy Clutter's room; his discomfort—rooted in jealousy—over Hickock's prostitute-seeking in Mexico; and his righteous indignation when Capote provided Hickock with girlie magazines on death row. Capote addressed the last matter. It occasioned, even Capote admits, a "tremendous falling-out" that lasted two months. Perry accused Capote of contributing to the degeneracy of Hickock's mind. He "got very grand." He "wouldn't speak or even write to me." For Capote, Smith's fury was still more evidence of his basic Puritanism. For Maloney it was sexually driven.

As for Smith and Capote, Maloney doubted the guards let Capote into Smith's cell. After all, on death row the rooms are open-faced (with plywood partitions between them). Outside the cell bars, however, one can hear guards coming; they don't just materialize out of the blue, unexpectedly. And that being the case, Capote and Smith "could have sex *through the bars*"—a practice common in American prisons, Maloney asserted, and one safely shielded from view. This was, in fact, Maloney's contention. He called it "entirely possible." He claimed Capote was "known to give blowjobs in parking lots and other odd places." He also cited as evidence the fact that, shortly before Smith was to be hanged, he kissed Capote on the cheek. "It's the only time," Maloney said, "I've ever heard of a condemned man doing such a thing." It's altogether surprising, no doubt; a jarring intimacy that is endlessly suggestive. But does it mean what Maloney thought it means? Even he was not certain. Still, sex or no sex, Maloney insisted that *In Cold Blood* reeked of Capote's love for Perry. Capote—"in the tortured logic peculiar to those in love"—blamed Hickock for Perry's predicament.

Maloney blamed Smith, who reacted to Hickock's aborted rape of Nancy by killing the Clutters, Nancy included.

No one ever claimed Capote had the greatest judgment. Maybe, as Clarke said, the rebellious child who was always there had usually been kept in check "by an adult of exceptionally clear vision." Then again, maybe not. Maybe, as Capote explained, there were always two people inside him—one intelligent, imaginative, mature; the other a fourteen-year-old. In some situations the adult was in control, in others, the adolescent.

I don't think Capote and Smith had sex. It's just the sort of reductive, simplistic possibility that entices those prepared to "go there"; the stuff of Hollywood movies. But whether between bars or clutching in the paid-for privacy of a death row cell, the notion is preposterous. I think Capote and Smith *talked about* their attraction to one another, openly acknowledged it, *fantasized* about it; I think there was closeness, sympathy, maybe even a form of love based on mutual recognition. But the relationship never got physical, beyond that gallows peck. The gallows peck was the one and only "sexual" act, a symbol of affection, nothing more. I should add: I've been alone in interview rooms with psychotic killers. In such instances, rapport—however deep, however genuine—provides miniscule reassurance. One thought replaces all others: Will this person try killing me, too? The order of the day is fear. Attraction, if it's even there, comes last. Capote knew one thing for certain: Smith was a killer. It was in his blood. He was psychotic, dissociated, unhinged. For him, murder was easy. It came naturally. It required no motive. The idea that Capote might simply shove such knowledge aside, put fear on dangerous hold, prance blithely and obliviously into a position of extreme vulnerability makes little sense. Yes, because of his childhood rejections, he searched out love wherever he might find it. Lovers consoled him, mothered him, fathered him, muted his entrenched anxieties. But from a crazy killer? Capote was reckless, but not *that* reckless. Besides, he was working on a masterpiece. The book meant immeasurably more than a feckless quickie.

There wasn't sex, I believe, but there was obviously something psychologically complex at work in the relationship. The Deweys both commented on Capote's feelings for Smith. Marie said he was "very fond" of Perry; Alvin, that he "saw himself" in Smith—same childhoods, same height, same build. Joe Fox, one of Capote's editors at Random House, was even more emphatic: "He adored Perry. Perry was a sort of doppelganger, of course."

The sympathy Capote felt for Smith was narcissistic. I don't mean that in any arcane, clinical sense. What I mean is that Capote saw Smith as a self-extension, a second, especially wayward, rage-filled possible self. A doomed alter-ego: the sum of an equation that could have been Capote's too. The technical term for this kind of process is *projective-identification*, a tool indispensable for artists, and one at Capote's constant disposal. He kept putting himself into Smith—like he did with Holly, Grady McNeil, Joel, Randolph, and others—and identifying with him more and more. Fox was correct: Smith *was* a doppelganger in the classic sense of the word: a double, a look-alike, a "bilocation," but a harbinger of bad luck, portending illness or danger. An omen of death. Smith was a "fetch" (the doppelganger's Irish version); Capote's self-creation. Even the yellow parrot could have been more Capote's fantasy than Perry's.

There's a less folkloric term for this phenomenon. Carl Jung called it the *shadow*, an "inferior function," that side of ourselves we don't dare express. Forbidden impulses, rejected thoughts and feelings, repellent fantasies—all get exiled to a shadowland where they form a virtually ancestral personality-in-waiting. For Jung, the goal of life is balance, a totality of Self (another such creation). Achieving unity requires shadow-confrontation. In fact, it is the very first step.

The shadow self has to be known; it has to be acknowledged and assimilated. It cannot be held at bay forever. If we ignore it or deny it, it only agitates more restively. It whispers, then speaks out loud, then howls till we hear. It might appear in dreams, it might appear in art, it might appear in symptoms, but most commonly it shows itself in relationships. We get to know the shadow by projecting it on other people, who then mirror it back to us. Seeing them, getting close to them, sympathizing with them is tantamount to shadow-exploration. Perry Smith, in Jungian terms, was Capote's projected shadow. And according to this line of thought, what Capote did with Smith was *healthy*. It was a form of self-enlargement. It was a reclaiming of darker, subterranean tendencies that were always there but never, to this point, sufficiently attended to. Smith was an opportunity. Capote opened himself up to the daemonic.

But less healthily, far more depressingly, because of the circumstances behind their affiliation, the pairing's outcome was assured. It was the "ouch" script from day one. Capote was fated to create a dark self; he was going to love his shadow projection, and the "fetch" was going to die. Yet another lost love, another abandonment, another punishment for misdirected intimacy. And this time, Capote literally watched it happen.

After appeal upon appeal, delay upon delay, the executions were carried out on April 14, 1965. Capote was in a serious state. To anyone who wanted to know, he said essentially the same thing: "It was the worst experience of my life. Period." Worse, then, than his mother's suicide. Worse than the hotel room lock-in. Worse than all of it. When Perry died, a bit of Capote died, too. He finished the book, but in a sense he *didn't* finish it. It was always the "echo that's meaningless and yet there: one keeps hearing it all the time." It "keeps churning around in my head," he said one year later. *In Cold Blood* was, he knew, "something I will never really get over."

Both Hickock and Smith wanted Capote there.[5] It was their most fervent desire. They also wanted Harper Lee, a more bizarre request. Lee declined. Capote almost did, too. He was divided on the subject. He made the trip to Kansas, bringing along a friend, Joe Fox, for emotional support, but at the eleventh hour he backed out. He called McAtee at 2:00 P.M. to say he was too emotionally distraught. He didn't think he could do it. But around 9:00 P.M. he changed his mind. He would see Hickock and Smith in their last few hours on earth, and he would also watch them die. He felt he had to. The book required it. He bit the bullet for the art.

Hickock also saw his former wife, a neat, well-groomed, well-spoken woman, "the last person in the world you'd think would be his wife," according to McAtee. It was a five-minute meeting, Hickock out of handcuffs so he could eat the shrimp he had requested as a final meal. Smith had no one, only Truman. He worried over what he might say. Should he apologize? And to whom? Could what he did really be undone with an apology? He wrote a poem about raising his eyes above walls of gray and going on his merry way. (Of course, to most in attendance, where Smith was going would be anything but merry.)

The executions took place in a literal warehouse, nothing at all like the high tech, custom-designed death chambers one hears about nowadays. There were no chairs. Everyone—about 20 people in all—stood. Building materials were stacked about the floor, lumber and the like. The floor was dirt, not even concrete. The building was dimly lit. There was a light rain. Somewhere a dog wailed mournfully, eerily, a doom-inflected hell-hound.

---

5. Under the statutes, the condemned men could select three witnesses.

Hickock went first, saying something about going to a better place, hoping people could forgive him. Morbidly, there were exactly thirteen steps to climb. A hood was placed over his head, the noose around his neck. He was hanged until the doctor on hand pronounced him dead. This official, final declaration often took as long as 30 minutes. Any gurgle or spasm signified lingering life.

A full hour after Hickock's death, Smith assumed the position. He climbed the steps with the prison chaplain. At one point he noticed, guiltily, that he was chewing gum, Juicy Fruit. He stepped over to Chaplain Post and spat it in his palm. His final words to Capote, whose cheek he kissed, were unexceptional, a simple "Adios, amigo."[6]

It is odd—very odd, in fact—but people tell diverging stories about Capote's behavior as Smith was hanged. Nye said Capote ran out of the building. He would not witness it. He saw Hickock die, Nye claimed, but not Smith. (This "fact" Nye cited as evidence for his notion that Capote and Smith were lovers). Tony Jewell, a reporter, said he stood next to Capote, but that they did not talk, and he did not note Capote's reaction. McAtee was aware of Capote's presence, but that was all. Bennett Cerf (Random House co-founder), who was not on hand, said Capote ran behind stacks of lumber and vomited. "I don't recall that at all," McAtee declares. In the end, it's a neat object lesson in the fallibility or subjectivity of memory, especially under conditions of trauma. We recall what we want to, not what happened. Capote's friend Joe Fox, who actually met Smith and Hickock in their final hours (much to the consternation of the cancer-stricken prison warden), flew with Truman back

---

6. At least, this was the story Capote told most often. But to Lawrence Grobel many years later, he said Perry's final words were "Goodbye. I love you and I always have."

home to New York. "He held my hand and cried most of the way. . . . Sobbing. It was a long trip."

In some ways, Capote never really got home. A bit of Kansas, and Smith, stayed in him forever. He came to understand, he said, that death is the "central factor" of life. That simple comprehension altered his entire perspective. *In Cold Blood* was a turning point, a climacteric moment. It was "the most emotional experience" of his creative life. But the darkened hallway he now found himself in was about to get inestimably darker. In his moment of unraveling, of losing his grip, he did the opposite of lying low. He upped the ante. He rolled loaded dice. He turned his attentions to a book that really would kill him: *Answered Prayers*. The shadow Perry Smith helped to liberate was soon to be given explicit, scorching voice.

5 | FRYING FANCY FISH

In Cold Blood was Capote's answered prayer, the masterpiece he eagerly anticipated. But it also proved the sentiment behind the phrase's putative origins: "More tears are shed over answered prayers than unanswered ones." The book was an enormous critical and financial success. It made $6 million in the mid-1960s, which, according to the most conservative of indices, amounts to roughly $36 million today. So Capote was wealthy like never before. He had been well off before, but not *this* well off. And the critics generally loved the book. "The best documentary account of an American crime ever written," said *The New York Review of Books*. "A masterpiece," *The New York Times Book Review* declared. The latter even threw in a little psychobiography: "There are two Truman Capotes," Conrad Knickerbocker wrote. "The artful charmer, prone to the gossamer and the exquisite,. . . and the darker and stronger discoverer of death." The word "stronger" is interesting in light of a comment by Norman Mailer, who felt that *In Cold Blood* actually achieved something no one else ever could, Lillie Mae included. It fortified Capote's masculinity. After he finished it, his effeminacy diminished noticeably. This was Mailer's take, at least. Death and murder magically made Capote a man. I have my doubts.

Mailer was one of the few who didn't like the book. His position was that Capote, never a big thinker, never one to grapple with difficult, complex ideas, glossed over all the questions that ought to keep one up at night. "It was too stripped down. . . . It was too behavioristic. . . . Truman decided too quickly this is all heredity, that in their genes his killers were doomed."

Others were more personal. Kenneth Tynan smelled blood—on the hands of the killers, and on Capote's too. He felt Capote could have done more to save Smith and Hickock; he might have stepped in with advice or money to get the death sentences overturned (Capote opposed capital punishment). Clarke calls Tynan's thesis sloppy, full of false assumptions about Kansas law at the time, "which would not have permitted the psychiatric defense Tynan was suggesting." Capote was coarser, as usual. The "table-turning" script kicked in as it always did when Capote found himself under attack, real or perceived. He wrote a long rebuttal to Tynan, a man possessing, in Capote's argot, "the morals of a baboon and the guts of a butterfly."

But the butterfly had a stinger. Capote was hurt by Tynan's accusations; they threw him into a weeks-long rage, diluting all the "masterpiece" talk. And prizes never came, either. No National Book Award, no Pulitzer: one judge making the case that the book was too commercial and therefore undeserving. A preposterous notion, but still it prevailed. Capote was characteristically neurotic when it came to awards. With bitter delight he ran them down, eviscerating untalented past winners like Pearl Buck (his favorite target); but secretly he yearned for recognition. Academics disgusted him, but he wanted their approval more than he could comfortably admit. He never would allow himself to look weak, at least not in the eye of the public. He pretended to be far stronger, far more impervious than he was. To the end the so-called "discoverer of death" was more gossamer than manly.

Literary feuding was one thing; life itself another. Capote was in no denial about the degree to which *In Cold Blood* had "scraped" him. "Before I began it I was a stable person," he said, comparatively speaking. "Afterward, something happened to me." The "something" included lashings of pills and alcohol. As he wrote the book his drinking grew exponentially; he needed booze to come down, to mute his anxiety, agitation, and impatience. A friend said, "He would start with a double martini, have another with lunch, then a stinger afterwards. That kind of drinking was new for him." His driver's license got taken away. Friends dropped him off at home, at the end of a long driveway (he insisted on walking from there). By spring of 1966, Cecil Beaton was predicting that Capote, a real neurotic case, "may not last long."

Adding to his troubles were several public appearances in which Capote was, to put it simply, hammered. He gave a talk at Towson State University in Maryland. Or, he tried to. He got yanked after five minutes: officials claiming he was drunk and mumbling obscenities. Worse by far was his appearance on the Stanley Siegel show in July, 1978. Capote was incoherent. He had a hard time even formulating words; his speech, when productive, incredibly slurred. Some claim Capote was okay when he arrived for the interview, but that he quickly popped a Thorazine in the studio.[1] Siegel stopped the interview after 17 sad, disturbing minutes. "What's going to happen unless you lick this problem of drugs and alcohol?" Siegel asked. "The obvious answer," Capote said, "is that eventually I'll kill

---

1. It's stunning that Capote even possessed Thorazine, an incredibly powerful anti-psychotic. When first introduced, the drug was called "a chemical lobotomy."

myself." Not the sort of innocuous chatter one expects from a talk show. Capote was clearly unglued.

Like everything does, the breakdown must have happened for a number of reasons combined. The writing was very hard, for one, and Capote's nerves were shot. There were myriad health issues, always depressing. Through the 1970s, Capote endured bursitis, pleurisy, an eye hemorrhage, bronchial pneumonia, and seizures during which he blacked out, once attacking a hotel employee. Perry's gruesome death must have also figured into Capote's distress. It is one thing, after all, for a close friend to die. It is another to watch him be hanged. The emotional effects of that particular image can hardly be calculated. And finishing *In Cold Blood*, practically a decade in the making, was also a kind of death. When a period of intense creativity reaches its conclusion, there is a dropping off of energy, a sense of loss. The obsession necessary for the work's success vanishes abruptly, leaving a void. For a long time there was *something*, always there, always distracting the mind, demanding solutions to creative problems; then there was *nothing*. Capote returned to himself, his life, who he was. He was a changed man, perhaps, but also much the same, with the same needs, the same fears, the same deep insecurities. What he usually did, from his youth, was write himself out of the hole. His problems found expression in fiction. He ejected them imaginatively, displaced them into the work.

So Capote soldiered on, broken, spent, frequently drunk and in and out of detox facilities, intermittently on Antabuse, feeling like "an insolvable jigsaw puzzle." Way back in 1958, right around the time *Breakfast at Tiffany's* appeared, Capote had imagined a *magnum opus*, the sort of book *In Cold Blood* became eight years later. It was very hush-hush, a project about which "I must be very silent," he wrote, "so as not to alarm my 'sitters.'" He wanted to call it

Answered Prayers, and "if all goes well, it will answer mine." He described the book as "a novel" initially. In fact, it was a *roman à clef*, a "faction," a work depicting real life in a fictional facade.[2] In other words, more nonfiction narrative, a form Capote swore he'd never return to. But he did, more or less against his will. He hurled himself back in the ring, a wobbly fighter. This time, the place of murderers was taken by high- or café-society women, the filthy rich "swans" whose names littered gossip columns and by whose side he increasingly trotted. Capote was their confidant. He was an expert listener: keen, interested, sympathetic, a "catalyst," as one friend said. He made their lives entertaining. He made *them* entertaining, according to those who saw him in action.

One of the primary swans, Slim Keith, told this story. She and Truman were sitting casually on her bed, gossiping as usual, dropping names, spilling beans. Upon entering the bedroom and seeing the famous author, Keith's husband's jaw fell four feet. The two were introduced. "Hello, Big Daddy," Truman said. Later, after dinner, Truman was out of the room washing his hands. The husband decided, "Let's keep him. We can put him on the mantel."

This was Act Two, Capote's new avocation. He had become, in some people's eyes, a "professional adorable man." He was a Pekinese perched on a pillow—cute, combed, pint-sized, letting out cranky yelps now and then. Martinis chilled. The yachts floated. Bitchy rumors circulated freely. But Capote was no one's pocket Merlin. He had a plan. This was research. It was the exact opposite of death

---

2. Capote's characterization of the book fluctuated. He did, at times, call it a *roman à clef*. But at other times he dismissed that depiction, saying, "I'm not bothering to disguise anything. I'm laying it right on the line, and to me, it's a literary experiment," like *In Cold Blood*.

row, but Capote was gathering material all the same. The mantelpiece decoration was not about to sit pretty.

Making sense of *Answered Prayers* is a tough job on several levels. On one hand, the work is unique in Capote's *artistic* life. There is really nothing like it. On the other hand, it is a perfect summary of all those aspects of Capote's *psychological* life outlined thus far—his attachment insecurity, his two primary scripts, his conflicts surrounding Lillie Mae, and his use of the written word as a means of dealing with emotional problems. If one surveys what Capote said about the book as he worked on it, what emerges is a convoluted farrago of claims, needs, hopes, and intentions.

There is a sense, for starters, of obligation. Capote said he was born to write the book, adding, "It's the only true thing I know." Nobody else could have written it, he declared. "I owe it to God to achieve what I know I can." There was this other level, he explained, "the ultimate state of grace, and I have to get there."

There was boastfulness, too, an assertion of strength and power. In an address to other writers, Capote asserted, "Not one of them would have had the guts" to have written it. "I'm laying it right on the line." Even before excerpts from the work-in-progress appeared, Capote received calls from café-society friends and jet-set wannabes, many ending with the question "Am I in your book?" The prospect was simultaneously fearsome and flattering. "We'll fit you in," came the reply, with "coffins to measure." From the get-go, Capote made no bones about what he was up to, threatening dreadful disclosures and scandalous revelations.

Despite the fact that he talked the book up endlessly, in interviews and TV show appearances, and despite his apparent need to repay some debt, to be true to his God-given talents, Capote gradually tired of the *Answered Prayers* song and dance. He didn't want to think about it or discuss it. He also didn't want to *finish* it.

"It's become a way of life," he said. "The moment I give it up it's just like I took it out in the yard and shot it in the head, because it will never be mine again." What he wished to retain, it seems, was the power the book provided, the fear it incited. *Answered Prayers* was his ace in the hole; if he played it, there was nothing left. "I guess there comes a point," he admitted, "where you have to give up, you have to give something over. And I don't want to. We'll see."

It was an odd position to be in. He wanted to write the book and he didn't; he wanted to publish the book and he didn't. With *In Cold Blood*, to take just one example, Capote was a writer obsessed. He worked like a madman. He knew what he had and he couldn't wait to deliver. His letters constantly referred to his progress, the ambition and impatience palpable. He was "exhausted, spent, a nervous wreck," but there was never the slightest hint of reluctance, let alone of quitting. With *Answered Prayers* it was a completely different story. The book rarely figured in his letters. It was almost invisible. When he did see fit to bring the subject up, it was to declare his "weariness" of writing it "or <u>anything</u>" — "nothing very interesting in my life" he confided depressingly—with intermittent but not very believable references to recovering, in moments, his creative energy. *In Cold Blood* set the bar dauntingly high; Capote felt intense, mainly self-generated pressure to leap it but doubted that he could. He was like an athlete aiming for a repeat championship; but he had lost his nerve and his touch. Something else he did in the letters is telling: he exaggerated the manuscript's length. He estimated one segment to be around 42,000 words, a figure he repeated more than once. In fact, it was just half that. Capote knew he was up against it. But he kept pretending, threatening the release of "homemade bombs."

It was a real mess he was in, and it threw him into a real creative crisis. What he finally did, or said he did, was reread all he had ever written, looking for some lost nugget of meaning or inspiration. The past, he figured, might reveal a future direction. It was as if he hoped to re-find what was now missing. But what he discovered was not reassuring. The material never fully exploded; it was never realized; he was never working with more than half, sometimes only a third, of the powers at his command. He found his entire comprehension of writing altered, as was his "attitude toward art and life and the balance between the two." So he went back to the drawing board. He started from scratch. He committed to perfecting a form combining all he knew about writing, all he'd learned from nonfiction narrative, the novel, short stories, film scripts, novellas, plays. "My whole life," he finally concluded, "has been spent developing the technique, the style, to write [*Answered Prayers*]. . . . It's done in the very best prose style that I think any American writer could possibly achieve. That's all I claim, but it's a pretty high claim. . . . It's the *raison d'être* of my entire life."

These are bone-crushing standards. At his lowest creative ebb, Capote set himself what was truly a Shakespearean task: the perfect crystallization of all his artistry. He knew his inspiration was flagging. He knew he was in terrible shape mentally and physically. He was drunk and drugged up more days than not. But he returned to the same formula that worked wonders with *In Cold Blood*. He decided to invent a style. It's fiction, but it's not. It's a *roman à clef,* except not quite. Capote was whipping himself again, announcing his intentions in print for all to see. But this time no creative monster stirred, no beast rose up to meet the challenge. Capote gave what he had left, but it wasn't close to enough. What he needed was Whitman's "barbaric yawp"; what he managed was a murmur.

The sad fact is, there *was* no *Answered Prayers*. It never came. At least, it hasn't yet. For some, to this day, it is a matter unresolved. Did he or didn't he finish it? The book is a literary Sasquatch. It's the visage of the Virgin Mary buried in the texture of a cornflake—it exists according to one's capacity to believe it exists.

Theories abound. Some claim it's stashed in a safe deposit box somewhere. Some say it was seized by an ex-lover. Some contend Capote kept it in a locker in the Los Angeles Greyhound Bus terminal. Some recall Capote carting around a manuscript several inches high, wrapped in a paper bag. Others suggest they surreptitiously riffled through the pages, only to discover a "Missouri bankroll": a few pages of writing on top, empty pages beneath.

John Knowles is one of the few with a specific memory to draw on. He remembers when Capote came to his home in Nyack, New York, which Truman named the Tree House. At the time the place was three-quarters finished; one needed to take a stepladder up to the master bedroom. Capote made himself an innocuous-sounding "orange drink"—vodka and orange juice. And on that fateful day he brought along with him the manuscript for *Answered Prayers*. Knowles says Capote started to show it to him. He recalls seeing a lot of it, "much more" than the slight excerpts eventually committed to print. Capote suggested they both take a look, but Knowles begged off, "which was madness on my part because he was making a great concession by showing me something of a work-in-progress." Capote never repeated the offer. Still, sight mostly unseen, Knowles firmly believes Capote wrote "hundreds of pages," found the work no good in the end, and burned it.

Joanne Carson, in whose arms Capote died, subscribes to the safe deposit box theory. She even claims she had a key—but one with no number. Still more dramatically, she says Capote gave her the key on the morning of his death. Alan Schwartz mostly concurs: "Yes, I think there was a key. There was no clue as to what it did unlock, or if it did, what was inside. . . . We tried to track it everywhere. We couldn't. So we're left with that."

Answered Prayers may have been Carson's final gift to Capote, an illusion she shared and wouldn't let die. She refers to three sections she claims to have actually, personally read: a final chapter, "The Nigger Queen Kosher Cafe," about a place on Long Island; "Yachts and Things," about the symbolism and power of money; and "And Audrey Wilder Sang," which includes a vivid scene of suicide during which a woman on the telephone watches disinterestedly as a person jumps from the roof above. She "just continues talking" as the body drops.

Who knows, *Answered Prayers* may be out there somewhere. Another book Capote wrote and claimed to have destroyed, *Summer Crossing*, emerged posthumously, rescued from the trash by a stealthy house-sitter. I have my own ideas about *Answered Prayers'* fate. And like so much of what happened in Capote's personal and artistic life, they revolve around attachment, in particular a clash of alternating attachment strategies, hyperactivation and deactivation. It is a subject I will return to later. For now, let's focus on what we do know. Capote may not have completed the book, the hole he dug and dug may never have dropped him into the crowded streets of China, but he did squeeze out sparks. In the mid-1970s, "La Cote Basque, 1965" appeared in *Esquire* magazine, followed by "Unspoiled Monsters" and "Kate McCloud." These three segments of the larger Proustian masterpiece are all we know of what it was or what it was meant to be. What do they tell us?

They tell us, first off, that *Answered Prayers* was an exceedingly bitchy, nasty, corrosive work, with no precursors in Capote's *oeuvre*. *Other Voices* was lyrical, intentionally so; fantasy-prone, gothic, adolescent. *Tiffany's* was stripped down, unadorned, a relatively slight novella. *In Cold Blood* was restrained, controlled, its author invisible in the sense that Capote himself never appeared as a character. *Answered Prayers,* contrastingly, has Capote all over it. Sex, never much of a subject for Truman, is everywhere too, in graphic terms. The work is also surprisingly postmodern and self-referential—the sort of thing Capote might have detested had he seen it tried by any other writer.

In 1973, Capote intended to feature a female main character, age 19, who meets a 42-year-old man, her roommate's father. They have an affair, but he refuses to marry her, partly because he's already married, and partly because he's plotting to become the next Republican president of the United States. This girl never appears in the work that was published, nor does the plotline. Instead, we are treated to P.B. Jones, a person as far from a 19-year-old girl as one can get. "Jones" is clearly Capote. He's a writer, he was abandoned as a child, he finds himself running in café-society circles, lunching with the rich and famous—from Garbo to Jackie Kennedy—and to top it off, he publishes a critically maligned book titled "Answered Prayers and Other Stories." He is also described by one character, an obvious Tennessee Williams stand-in, as "innocent and injured"— a neat summary of Capote's basic psychological position in the world. As an "innocent," Capote got hurt—as in the "ouch" script. When injured, the tail of the rattler flared—as in the "table-turning" script.[3]

Clarke calls Jones Capote's "errant and amoral twin." He is, just like Perry Smith was. And though no one seems to have noticed this before, Jones is also Smith, a fact I'm certain Capote was aware of. At one point in the story Jones even goes by the name

---

3. Capote's position on Jones was ambiguous. He told Clarke, "P.B. isn't me, but on the other hand he isn't *not* me. His background is totally different"—not true—"but I can identify with it psychologically. I'm not P.B. but I know him very well." It's an unconvincing take. Capote even has the character P.B. photographed by Cecil Beaton for his first book's back cover—a similar come-hither shot of Truman appeared with *Other Voices*.

of Smith, becoming "P. Smith." (We never learn what the "P" stands for.) But Jones also shares Perry's history—he was raised in an orphanage by Catholic nuns, but he is conniving and duplicitous, "a kind of Hershey bar whore—there wasn't much I wouldn't do for a nickel's worth of chocolate." In short, Jones has no morals, a fact Capote states more than once. He's a sociopath, like Perry Smith, prone to thievery and check-forging. There's even a physical resemblance. Jones is on the short side, five feet seven, sturdy and well-proportioned.

So P.B. Jones was Capote's clever way of keeping Perry Smith alive, dropping him, in fact, into a world he'd never known, never dreamed of knowing. Smith's death wounded Capote emotionally; in fiction he resurrected him, performed imaginary CPR. It was almost as if Capote arranged Smith's revenge against a universe of elites who never looked twice at him. It was a debt to a friend Capote may have felt he owed. Anyway, he pulled it off. The jet set proves little match for P.B.'s guile, his native opportunism. He has a veritable field day.

The plot is difficult to summarize because the three pieces do not particularly cohere; there is little sense of a whole, a narrative arc. The reader simply follows Jones around peripatetically, privy to one scandalous and/or sex-perfused adventure after another. His book dead on arrival, Jones becomes a masseur, then works for "Miss Self" as a male gigolo. All his clients are men. There's an especially vicious portrait of Tennessee Williams (not named outright but easily recognizable), one of Jones's assignations, whose large bulldog Jones blithely allows to "rape" him in a park for all to see (and many do). Williams has a "corn-pone" voice; he's a most acclaimed American playwright. He has no friends because the only people he pities are his characters and himself—"everyone else is an audience." Just like one of his adrift heroines, he "seeks attention and sympathy by serving up half-believed lies to total strangers." Williams at last tells Jones to "roll over and spread those cheeks." Sorry, but I don't catch, Jones replies. No matter, says Williams, "I don't want to corn-hole you, old buddy. I just want to put out my cigar." Jones high-tails it out of the room.

Jones is bisexual, but for him, sex is never an expression of love; it's a way of getting what he wants out of people. He has it only when he must. And it's always ugly. He manages to meet, for instance, a writer named Alice Lee Langman. What he wants from her is an agent, a publisher, a "Holy Roller critique" of his work in some august publication (all of which he achieves). The woman is a talker with no sense of humor. When the two have sex, Jones endures a running heated-up commentary ("Jesus have mercy, Jesus Jesus," etc.) followed by "a sixty second sequence of multiple triumphs." He then repairs to the bathroom to masturbate, dredging up whatever useful images come to mind. (He does the same thing later with a different female character.) Reflecting there alone, he recalls the words of a friend approvingly: "The only women I've got any use for are Mrs. Fist and her five daughters."

This misogyny is a theme. It arises directly out of Capote's childhood with Lillie Mae. Women are either idealized or detested. As an instance of the former, there is Kate McCloud, who hires Jones as a paid companion; some believe her ex-husband plans to kill her. In a weirdly masturbatory paragraph, Capote describes her "quivering" breasts, the "perfection of her posture," her "brilliant eyes," her "fascinating hair" (Can hair really be fascinating?) She requires no make-up, her pleasingly pouted lips possessing a pinkness all their own. Ostensibly, Jones is massaging her. He does, briefly. Then he gets an annoying, distracting, "unprofessional" hard-on, a problem resolved like before with Langman.

McCloud is a Southern girl, like Nina. Self-made and shrewd, like Nina, she's plotting to move up in society. She also has a five-year-old son whom she adores, whom she lives for, who was taken from her by her husband (Capote went to live with the Faulk sisters right around the same age). She imagines perhaps kidnapping him, and Jones fantasizes doing the job as a way of making her love him. McCloud is Nina improved, idealized. She does not leave her son, he's taken from her. And all she can think of is getting him back—a wish crossing Nina's mind at best intermittently, at worst never.

But McCloud is an exception in the *Esquire* excerpts. Far more frequently, women are attacked in language that's unsparing. An agent, Margo Diamond, is a "pockmarked muffdiver," a "slit-slavering bitch." Troubled socialite Barbara Hutton (no pseudonym), whose mother committed suicide—Barbara found her dead—and who married seven times, once to Cary Grant, is a "dime-store maharini," with a "vacancy often observed in people long imprisoned." Art collector and sometime patron Peggy Guggenheim appears in passing (no pseudonym); to Capote she resembles "a long-haired Bert Lahr." Even Jackie Kennedy (no pseudonym) gets it good. Far less beguiling than her sister Lee, in Capote's estimation, she looks for all the world like a "female impersonator impersonating Mrs. Kennedy." The list goes on and on. Capote liberated quite a fund of fury, and just like he said he would, he was laying it on the line. *Women are like rattlesnakes; the last thing that dies is their tail*, says Capote at one point in the narrative. It sums up Jones's outlook in a sentence.

With mostly pseudonym-free, scorching dismissals like these—the above representing a heavily truncated sampling—it's no wonder at all that the "swans" Capote cultivated and in some cases truly loved—the C.Z Guests, Gloria Vanderbilts, and Babe Paleys of the world—reacted with stricken outrage, instantly blacklisting him. "La Cote Basque, 1965," another *Answered Prayers* installment, quickly set the socialite world on fire, with reactions ranging from, in Capote's fake-carefree words, "the insane to the homicidal."

It begins with two cowboys discussing "jacking off," then proceeds to the setting of the famed restaurant, where all the action occurs. But there isn't any action per se. Jones simply lunches with Lady Ina Coolbirth, who needs someone to dish to. And dish she does. Immediately Harry Cohn, president of Columbia Pictures, appears—he's a "sleazy Hollywood hood" who, upon learning that Sammy Davis, Jr., was dating his blond star Kim Novak, erupts, "Listen, Sambo, you're already missing one eye. How'd you like to try for none?"

The stories keep flying. Cole Porter unzips the fly of a nut-brown wine steward, hauls out and shakes his penis. Carol Matthau—Walter's wife—speaks of "stealing sleeping pills out of other people's medicine cabinets" and stockpiling them in order to bump herself off. The Kennedy men are "like dogs, they have to pee on every fire hydrant." "Old bugger" Joe Kennedy comes in for special abuse. Coolbirth describes how, on one occasion—when she was eighteen, a guest in the house—he slipped into her bedroom at six in the morning and assaulted her— "one hand over my mouth and the other all over the place, right there in his own house with the family sleeping all around us."

The longest anecdote concerns Ann Woodward (whom Capote calls Ann Hopkins). Woodward, née Crowell, was an actress and showgirl in New York nightclubs. She met William Woodward, Jr., heir to the Hanover National Bank fortune, sometime during World War II, when he fought in the Navy, receiving a medal for bravery. The two married in 1943, to his family's extreme displeasure. There were two sons.

Never especially happy, the marriage ended scandalously in October, 1955. There had been reports of prowlers targeting nearby estates, so the couple, both avid hunters, repaired to separate rooms with loaded shotguns ready. Hours later, thinking she heard noises in the home, Ann tiptoed out, weapon in hand. She fired at what she believed to be an intruder, in fact killing her husband. Ann was never charged, but the story became a *cause célèbre*. In a ghastly aftermath, both sons committed suicide by jumping from windows.

Capote, of course, tells his own virtually undisguised version of this depressing tale in *Answered Prayers* through mouthpiece Lady Coolbirth. He throws in a handful of ruthless characterizations of Woodward, who once apparently called him "a fag," a mistake she'd live (just barely) to regret. He describes her as a tramp, "always a tramp," brought up in some "country-slum way" in West Virginia, a "dangerous serpent," a "white-trash slut," married and divorced twice, working as a call girl for a bell-captain pimp at the Waldorf, when fortune smiled on her and she met "David Hopkins," her future husband, a biggie she knew she'd hooked and who was soon "writhing inside the grip of [her] expert Cleopatra's clutch." Ann is a clever social climber, her pickup incredibly quick. She learns to ride. She studies French. She gets up to speed on furniture, fabrics, and modern painting, campaigning in her free time (and there is a lot of it) for the "Best Dressed List." She's a Holly Golightly absent the heart of gold, absent the basic innocence.

But her amorousness does her in. In real life Capote nicknamed Woodward "Bang-Bang"; in *Answered Prayers,* he has her "racing her motor in the Grand Prix manner," known by every male past puberty as "Madame Marmalade"—her favorite *petit dejeuner* "hot cock" lathered in strawberry jam. Her husband hears whispers of infidelity and hires a private detective to see what he can dig up. Soon there are Polaroids of Ann "being screwed front and back by a couple of jockeys in Saratoga." The deal is sealed when the detective also discovers she's still legally the wife of "hillbilly jarhead" Billy Joe Barnes.

Ann, realizing the jig is up, knowing her husband has her "by the snatch," hatches a final scheme. She spies shadowy, black-clad prowlers that don't really exist, makes repeated fake-terrified calls to police, then uses the prowler excuse to murder her husband—in the shower, no less, a spot few un–brain-damaged prowlers seek out urgently. She gets off, abetted by her husband's mother—who fears the tarnish of a trial—and comes away clean with her portion of the family fortune secure.

There's Golightly in Ann; there's also Nina, down to the last Southern-gothic, social-climbing detail. Words were always weapons for Capote, from the days of "Busybody." But this time they were lethal. Woodward, already depressed and unstable, read a smuggled advance copy of "La Cote Basque, 1965" and swallowed a fatal dose of Seconal—the same drug, as fate would have it, that killed Nina Capote. So in this case, more than any other, the "table-turning" script reached a terrible apex. Capote's art essentially murdered a woman guilty of nothing more heinous than calling him a fag. And as for Ann's mother-in-law? "Well, that's that," she said. "She shot my son, and Truman just [killed] her, and so now I suppose we don't have to worry about that anymore." Apparently Capote wasn't the only heartless character in the sordid drama.

Woodward's reaction was the first, by far the saddest and most anguished, but hardly the last. Capote's swans barked and recoiled: he was dead to them in a New York minute. It is stunning how swift and how implacable the response was, in fact. Capote made calls—or had others make calls for him as he listened fearfully on a second line—and wrote letters, but two of the women whose friendship he enjoyed most—Slim Keith and Babe Paley—never spoke to him again. The curtain fell, and that was it. The finality of their dismissal, its completeness, floored Truman, rejection being the one thing, given his life history, he always said he "despised in all forms." Keith's and Paley's response also suggests how superficial the friendship was to begin with—at least from the women's perspective (Capote's too, it would seem). They dropped Capote without misgiving, with no sense of loss, guilt, or sadness.

Slim Keith, the model for Coolbirth, the character dishing most of the gossip in "La Cote Basque, 1965," was "absolutely undone," appalled that Capote "could be sitting across from me at a table and then go home and write down everything I had said." She adored him, she claimed, but she was repulsed by his use of their friendship and by "my own bad judgment." Keith "looked on Truman as a friend who had died. . . . I took the cleaver and chopped him out of my life."

"That dirty little toad is never coming to one of my parties again," snarled Nedda Logan, enraged by Capote's acid portrayal of her soirées. Gloria Vanderbilt claimed she would spit on him if she ever saw him again. Babe Paley, to whom Capote wrote two long explanatory letters, spoke of him with "total loathing," according to mutual friend John Richardson. He was a "snake who had betrayed her." Even fellow writer and erstwhile friend Tennessee Williams, who came in for harsh treatment, had anything but forgiveness in mind: "The thing Capote has written is shockingly repugnant and thoroughly libelous. . . . [He's] a monster of the first order, a cold-blooded murderer at heart." Katharine Anne Porter, disguised slightly in *Answered Prayers* as Alice Lee Langman, the writer "Jones" screws opportunistically, called the book "unspeakably hideous." Apparently, she said, Capote's life had "turned into a kind of poison that he's spitting out over the world. I don't know why." "He's destroying himself," another writer, Ned Rorem, said. "Where can he go from here?"

Good question. A magazine title, "Is Truman Human?" summed the situation up brilliantly. Porter said he was from "another planet," his judgment utterly incomprehensible. So we arrive now at the psychological question lurking behind every page of this book. Why did Capote (almost) write *Answered Prayers*? What "crazy wind" possessed him? It's true, in relation to his previous work, that the book is anomalous, a definite outlier. But it's also predictable, a development in perfect keeping with who he was and how he went about regulating an emotional life that was always tenuously controlled at best.

Nobody ever does anything for just one reason—that's a cardinal assumption of work in psychobiography. Motives are *overdetermined*, more chorus than solo, comprising groups of voices singing simultaneously, though not necessarily harmoniously. Networks of needs combine adventitiously to bring about action, or dreams, or feelings. To get at what Capote was after with *Answered Prayers*, it's essential to survey a wide field of mostly hidden intentions, but the starting point is attachment, the *leitmotif* of Capote's life.

Capote was insecurely attached—we know that for sure. He developed two alternating strategies for dealing with fear and anxiety: hyperactivation and deactivation. His attachment system was stuck in red-alert mode. He needed love and support desperately; it shored him up when it came, and he monitored carefully, almost automatically, the degree of attentiveness aimed his way. These are hyperactivating strategies; their aim is to keep love around. But for those insecurely attached, any momentarily pleasing status quo is fragile. It can disappear in a heartbeat. Thus, as Capote once explained, "If I feel somebody has betrayed me or been disloyal about something, I get terribly upset about it." Or, "I despise rejection." Or, in answering a question about whether the rich really are so different from the non-rich, "Yes, [they are]. They're more disloyal. The rich run together, no matter what."

Capote's number-one fear, he always said, was abandonment. Love was problematic; it didn't stick around. His faith in it chronically wavered. Long before "La Cote Basque, 1965," back when Capote's status with socialites seemed quite a bit more secure, he told Slim Keith, "I love you very much, Big Mama." I love you too, Truman, she replied. It went back and forth: "No, you don't." "Yes I do." "How can you say that? People don't love me," Capote objected. "I'm a freak."

A tiny exchange, but telling all the same. These were women whose orbit Nina aspired to occupy. Many of them were self-made too—they climbed the ladder with tenacity of purpose and reached the top. But Nina's example spread to the swans. She was a betrayer; they might be, too. The threat was omnipresent. And Capote came to detest the mascot role, the *contingent* responsiveness it entailed. "I don't particularly like rich people," he confessed at last. "In fact, I have a kind of contempt for them. . . . Really rich people are the most pathetic, so frightened, so insular. A yacht and five houses is what they have in common. . . . Like a bunch of bees in a beehive, all they really have is their money." Money is what they love, Capote implied. Then added: "They don't even like each other."

With *Answered Prayers*, then, Capote doubled down on a hyperactivating strategy that must have seemed practically perfect: *preemptive abandonment*. He set café society on fire in order not to get burned. And it worked. He wasn't rejected (at least not in his way of figuring things). He wasn't abandoned. He wasn't a victim. He was a *victimizer*. He was in command, and they were under his large thumb. All they could do was squirm, protest, and call him names. The dogs might bark, but the caravan moved on. Capote had the power to tell as many tales as he wished to, to betray as many confidences as he liked. It was his decision, his choice. Not theirs. He set the terms. The relationships were in his hands.

Preemptive abandonment was Capote's strategy, probably largely unconsciously, without clear awareness or insight; and equally unconsciously, he made it P.B. Jones's too. Early on we get Jones's backstory—his abandonment in the balcony of a vaudeville theater, his life in an austere, red-stone orphanage overlooking the Mississippi River. He was "bright" and a "beauty," a genius, a favorite of the nuns, one of whom, Sister Martha, an English teacher, he "rather liked." The two were close; she felt he had a gift for writing, so much so that "I became convinced of it myself." But she underestimated his innately conniving, duplicitous nature. And when Jones took off, hitchhiked with no particular destination in mind, he didn't "leave her a note or even communicate with her again." A "typical sample," he allows, "of my numbed, opportunistic" personality. A perfect example, too, in the fiction, of preemptive abandonment. Later Jones is even more forthcoming, philosophizing languidly about his basic tendencies: "I didn't say goodbye to anybody; just left." He is the type, he muses, by no means rare, "who might be your closest friend, a buddy you talked to every day, yet if one day you neglected to make contact, if *you* failed to telephone *me*, then that would be it, we'd never speak again. . . . Just left, yes; sailed at midnight. . . ." Capote's real life was leaking into the fiction's fantasy. With the system on constant red-alert, even oblique abandonment threats required immediate counter-measures: *You can't leave me because I'm leaving you first.* In fact, for Jones, love itself is a "horror," too risky to be entertained seriously. Life is actually "mutual exploitation." It isn't possible to really love when "your first interest is the use you can make of" another person.

The aim of attachment strategies is emotion-regulation. The prospect of anxiety, fear, depression, or loss instigates mitigating behavior. Preemptive abandonment is *not* emotion-denying; the fear is there, it's present, it's powerful. It just gets sidestepped. The bullet is dodged. But Capote tried hyperactivation's opposite, too. With *Answered Prayers* and its aftermath, it was all-defensive-hands-on-deck. Every resource was mobilized. It's a bit hard to believe (too much imperviousness to swallow), but in addressing expectations concerning the book, Capote declared: "I never think about it. I have a way of blocking things completely out of my mind and I have had since I was a child, because I've had a lot of things to block out of my mind. Things that create anxiety and apprehension and whatnot. . . . It's just as though I took some kind of magical pill. . . ." Then after the attacks from all sides, he said this, boastfully: "They can accuse me of mass murder and it wouldn't make my pulse skip a beat. I don't care about anything. You should never let them sense a weakness in you, because then they'll go for you like sharks."

These statements imply *deactivation*—emotion-suppression, emotion-denial. Nothing can touch him. He's beyond pain. He's beholden only to his art. He can't—and doesn't—think of consequences. The reality, of course, was more complex, deactivation more wish than fact. Capote feared hurt—he always did, it was the story of his life—but he was fearless (he claimed). He was plagued by anxiety and apprehension, but the magical pill of denial protected him. Working on *Answered Prayers* made Capote a "nervous wreck," he admitted. He tried the lubricant of cocaine but it only interfered in the long run. By 1977 he had a "nervous breakdown." Despite serious misgivings, he tried psychoanalysis, but it did him "absolutely no good whatsoever." There was talk of "writer's block"— his flow was gone, there was no urgency or inspiration to draw on. A lot of this, I believe, can be traced to conflicting strategies. In Capote's case, hyperactivation would call for relationship restoration, relationship damage-control as a means of assuaging the anxiety of loss. Deactivation is the exact opposite. There is no anxiety to assuage, there is no hurt. In short, no feeling at all, no relationship threat.

There are many reasons *Answered Prayers* remained unfinished. One is the fact that Capote himself was finished, creatively speaking. He just did not have it. It wasn't in him. *In Cold Blood* had drained the well. Alcoholism, too, tamped down his creative energies. But another reason concerns attachment. The magic pill wasn't so magic after all. Capote might have *claimed* obliviousness, he might have *said* he didn't care, but his history had caught up with him. In truth he was far more fragile than fearless.

Kate Harrington, the daughter of one of his lovers, John O'Shea, was there to see it all unfold. It was tragic, she says, like a death in the family. "He went into a colossal depression." He never got up again. There was heavy drinking and drugging. The phone stopped ringing. All was silence. "We sat for many, many weeks just hibernating. . . . He wouldn't get out of bed and the days would turn into nights; he never opened the blinds and I'd sit and we'd talk. He was so upset he'd cry, and he'd go in and out of that thing that someone does when they've done something tragic, where they have remorse." He thought they'd come back, Harrington says Capote told her. "I thought they'd be mad for a while." But they stayed mad, forever; they never came back, the relationships weren't restored. "He was staggered by that. . . . For two years he sort of went on, but it was never the same."

So much for stoicism. Princess Lee Radziwill, the erstwhile betrayer, also had a close-up view of Capote's deterioration. "He didn't understand he was being treated like a toy," she explained. He took to carrying around a doctor's black bag stuffed with pills he would crush and swallow with Scotch. "He needed to take tranquilizers. . . because he was an extremely nervous person. . ., much more tense than people realized, or than he appeared to be when he was trying to amuse everyone. I think his life was a strain every day." It was very depressing, Radziwill said; Capote came to stay for a while but the specter frightened the children. "He was no longer the Truman I knew."

But in many ways this was the same old Truman, just intensified, more vividly on display. *Answered Prayers* elicited attachment-based dilemmas; it also activated the familiar "table-turning" script, that set of feelings and behaviors Capote unleashed whenever he sensed he was being underestimated. He was a toy, a mantelpiece decoration, an amusing sidekick who listened well and gossiped better. Worse yet, he was innocuous, harmless. It was a role Capote came to detest, just as he came to detest the lifestyles and values of the rich and famous. The idea these swan socialites had of him duplicated the notion shared by neighbors and schoolteachers that he was not only different, but possibly retarded. Just like he turned tables on doubters by acing the IQ test as a child, he proved to the jet set that he was no mere blasé butterfly as an adult. He was a force; they needed to be made to know that. Who did they think they had, he kept repeating, who did they think I was? "They assumed that I was living by their values," Capote said. "Which I never was. It's as though, by writing that, I was saying to them, 'Everything you lived for, everything you did, is a lot of shit.' Which is true! I *was* saying that!"

A few of Capote's targets in *Answered Prayers* were anything but accidental. Ann Woodward had called him a fag, so she got hers. And William Paley, Babe's husband, got his too, because he put down and generally failed to appreciate Capote's swan *nonpareil*, the woman whose loss of friendship Truman felt most acutely. This was the perfect table-turning by proxy. Bill underestimated Babe; Capote adored Babe, so Bill was made to pay. In one of "La Cote Basque, 1965's" most salacious anecdotes, a Bill Paley stand-in seduces the ugly WASP wife of a governor simply because "she was the living incorporation of everything denied him, forbidden to him as a Jew, no matter how beguiling and rich he might be." The encounter ends disastrously, and Bill gets a lot more than he bargained for—he's humiliated, reduced to inferiority. Capote's lover O'Shea read the story in draft form and begged Capote to excise it. "I've never understood, and will never understand, why he put it in," says O'Shea. "There's something there that defies analysis."

Not really. It makes complete sense. Sell Capote short, or sell Capote's dear friend short, at your peril. Any such miscalculation was filed forthwith in the secret table-turning ledger. Capote consoled himself, pretty cavalierly, as it turned out, with the thought that Bill would never notice, never recognize himself. "[He's] too dumb," Capote mistakenly figured. He wasn't. And neither was Babe, the woman he thought he was standing up for.

Other targets make less sense. Montgomery Clift ("a great friend of mine"), Katherine Anne Porter ("an extremely good writer"), Dorothy Parker (who agreed with Capote when he called Kerouac's writing "typing"), and Tennessee Williams, who unlike playwrights Eugene O'Neill and Arthur Miller was actually "good," in Capote's view—all get pilloried to different degrees, Williams most painfully. What for? No table-turning seems to be in effect—though it's hard to say for sure—no preemptive abandonment seems necessary. The writer William Styron, whose work Capote always respected even on the rare occasions when critics demurred, found what Capote did "inexplicable," "disastrous." "If real people are our friends and we write about them in such a way to expose them, as Truman did, as bizarre and misbehaving and creepy and loony, then we can only expect some sort of retaliation. And he got it." In the end, Styron was inclined to regard *Answered Prayers* as "an act of willful destruction." George Page, host and narrator of the PBS series *Nature*, saw it as "very *self*-destructive." Capote always wanted to shock, Page said. Plus, "he must have been thinking that he couldn't write anymore." So he knocked himself off "his extraordinary social pedestal"—true social suicide, in short.

Styron and Page are both correct. There was destruction *and* self-destruction at work. What comes through most acidly as one reads the published excerpts is an encompassing feeling of disgust. Hatred, too, but of a *sensual* kind. The world depicted, the people who populate it—everywhere everything is unredeemable, sordid, venal, repugnant. It almost *smells* bad. By this time, with only a handful of years left to live, Capote was sick of himself more than anyone or anything else, and the sickness spread slimily, like an oil slick. He took pains to create a narrator he invested with his own worst characteristics. Jones is a snake, a liar, a user, a self-proclaimed genius whose single work—*Answered Prayers* no less—gets savaged by critics. He claims to want to write but never does. He hates himself but makes no apologies. He is who he is. A sociopath pseudo-artist. A faker.

The destructive element, as opposed to the self-destructive, was fueled by deeper motives. It was more repressed, more subtextual. There was the anger in table-turning and preemptive abandonment, but a sizeable portion of rage erupted out of the clotted, emotionally saturated *imago* of Lillie Mae/Nina. From the first, Lillie Mae was a swan wannabe. In fact, though she never achieved exalted status in the jet-set stratosphere, she was still Capote's first real swan, the prototype. The women Capote ran with were Nina's ideals, they hit the jackpot she could only dream of. Destroying them was destroying a more distilled, more crystallized version of her. Capote burned Nina in effigy.

There was a precedent for concealed Nina-hate in Capote's early fiction, too. The story "Miriam" is one of his most famous, though he didn't like it much, and found it too formulaic, too overwrought. The tale concerns a mysteriously motherless, sociopathic little girl who enters, then destroys, the life of a 61-year-old widow, Mrs. H. T. Miller. As Capote was to say later, the girl, in his interpretation, doesn't really exist. The old woman essentially hallucinates her, precipitating her descent into madness. I see a different reading, not necessarily contradictory. Miriam is Capote, and Mrs. Miller is Nina. Just like Truman as a child, Miriam is parentless. And as Mrs. Miller observes more than once, Miriam's mother, whoever she may be, must care little for her, especially in light of the fact that the girl arrives at the old woman's home at all hours of the night. "Your mother must be insane. . . . She must be out of her mind," the widow exclaims. Of course, as a child Capote experienced a similarly un-chaperoned freedom. His mother never knew where he was because she was never around.

Miriam's hair is "absolutely silver-white, like an albino's." Truman's hair was "snow white," he was a "tiny towhead pretty enough to be a girl." Miriam dresses with a special tailored elegance. Truman's mother "dressed him too well . . . and made him as conspicuous as Little Lord Fauntleroy." Capote's cousin Sook even made him up like a girl, "putting a bonnet on his head [Miriam wore a beret], wrapping a feathered boa around his neck, and fitting his feet into embroidered slippers." Miriam has a large vocabulary for such a small child, throwing around words like "moderately." Capote did too, by all accounts. And Miriam's strange exoticism mirrors Capote's. Both seemed spookily un-childlike, possessed of a luminous ethereality. In one of the story's first scenes, the moment when Miriam meets Mrs. Miller, the two attend a movie. One of Truman's teachers got in the habit of walking him home from school, stopping along the way at a theater.

As the plot advances, Miriam grows more and more irrepressible. She moves into the widow's room—sternly announcing "I've come to live with you"—steals her precious cameo brooch and hurls a vase filled with paper roses to the floor, then instructs Mrs. Miller to "kiss me good night" (the woman musters just enough strength to decline). The tale ends obscurely. The widow falls back hopeless and bleary while Miriam remains, eluding a neighbor's apparent pursuit. We aren't sure what the future may bring, though we expect the worst.

This is pure wish-fulfillment, thematically identical to Capote's attack against the mother-swans. But in "Miriam," the table-turning is more explicit. If Capote's mother never wanted him, then Miriam *makes* the widow want her, and the widow is pathetically powerless to say no. If, as Jack Dunphy maintains, Nina aimed to dominate a spirit she never understood, then Miriam is a spirit thoroughly indomitable, in fact dominating. And if Nina abandoned Truman, then Miriam/Capote is the mother-deprived castoff come home to exact revenge, to drive the capricious and crazy-making mother into abject insanity. Miriam won't take no for an answer. She deserves love, and she will get it. Period. Her power exceeds by far whatever reserves of strength the stricken widow might muster.

Capote couldn't love his mother but he couldn't *not* love her, either. He wanted her there and away at the same time. She was the black knot at the center of his life. Destroying the swans was a small unraveling, a liberation, yet it came at the cost of guilt. Capote denied regret, denied feeling altogether, but it was there. Destruction arrived ambivalently, in other words. And so, while Capote took deadly aim at various Nina stand-ins in *Answered Prayers*, he also came to his mother's defense. He had his cake and ate it, too. In her final years, before the fatal dose of Seconal in January, 1954, Nina was obsessed with being accepted by café society. She was on the brink, the dream near realized, when Joe Capote capsized the yacht—he was caught stealing cash to support a growing gambling habit. This looming disgrace, some feel, was more than Nina could bear. Her addiction to the jet-set lifestyle, the failure of her life's project, destroyed her. "'Somebody killed my mother.' That would be the question Capote must have asked himself almost on an unconscious level," literary archivist Andreas Brown hypothesizes. So Capote was filled with bitterness and a need for retribution, both of which got channeled into *Answered Prayers*. He "killed" the people who "killed" his mother.

"That whole thing of Nina's suicide affected Truman," says Phoebe Pierce Vreeland, who knew Nina well. "Like a crack in the foundation of a house. . . . It was central. . . . Truman had been in a way responsible for Nina and failed. In many ways Truman was the parent and she was the child."

Capote's contempt for the rich was multifaceted; but it gained momentum in the wake of Nina's loss. The lifestyle did her in. It was the lifestyle's fault, not Truman's. And if revenge was what, to whatever degree, lubricated Capote's efforts on the book, his heedlessness and obliviousness of the viciousness of the content seem fractionally less puzzling. He was a man on a mission. He *wanted* what he wrote to sting, he *wanted* it to hurt. At times he'd complain that those who attacked him for the book's content failed to understand what it was really about. Perhaps, in part, revenge for his mother's suicide was the mysterious X factor. Perhaps that's what nobody quite understood—nor could they.

It's funny, the book's title Capote found enormously captivating. Be careful what you wish for; you may want it less than you think. It fit him, but it fit Nina even better. What she prayed for—class status—she got, however marginally, but at the cost of her life.

In Cold Blood and the reaction to *Answered Prayers* were two body blows Capote couldn't absorb. The first was a surprise. Success floored him. It came and he veered. His devotion was gone, his work habits derailed. The impulse was spent. He'd achieved his masterpiece, and Act Two of his life must have seemed virtually imponderable. He threw his famous Black and White Ball, and the partying never stopped. Then there was Andy Warhol, Studio 54, cocaine, prescription pills, Stoli vodka in an unmarked glass. All the while, Perry Smith lingered. I don't think it's possible to trace the convoluted effects of that loss on Capote, but it rocked him to the core. He didn't recover. He pressed on, but fitfully, on a dark arc.

Answered Prayers, what there was of it, sealed his fate. Capote feigned surprise, but his indignation was hard to buy. The handmade bomb exploded, and Capote was left amid mere debris, not standing but teetering. He was right, it took guts to write the book, just as it takes guts to commit suicide. It ended the same way it all began. He was alone in his hotel room, locked in, hurt, wailing. The people who were supposed to have loved him were gone, out for a night on the town. He was dead to them, and he was dead to himself.

On one occasion, with Kurt Vonnegut, Capote passed out while walking outside to a lunch spread. His legs just buckled under him; Vonnegut caught his fall with the help of a nearby friend. Capote was used to this, he said. It was nothing new. "We were not to worry," Vonnegut says Capote insisted. "We were to lay him out." Eventually Vonnegut took him home. Like he always did in those days, Capote told him not to use the driveway. He would walk in, under his own power. "Afterward," Vonnegut says, "we all wondered if he really had had it."

John Knowles recalls another evening when Capote nearly died. He'd somehow lost $4,000 worth of cocaine in Knowles's front yard, and he spent quite a bit of time looking for it, unsuccessfully. When he returned to the house, he didn't know where he was. He seemed not to know who Knowles was, either: "He looked at me. . . . I was suddenly a very menacing version of myself. A really menacing person."

Somehow Knowles got Capote into bed in the guest room, but he kept falling out. Fifteen times or more, Knowles estimates. He'd hear a crash, get Capote back to bed, then hear another crash—on into the night. "He was doing ghastly mixings of things," Knowles remembers. "His breathing became terribly thin, long gasps in his breathing."

There were frequent, probably drug-induced or alcohol-induced hallucinations. Capote saw robbers in the house, taking his jewels, stealing his cash. The emerging epilepsy (or seizures, at least), Knowles believes, was self-inflicted—a result of chronic abuse of the nervous system, far too much drinking and drugging. There were many more instances of fainting. Capote passed out in the UN Plaza. He passed out in the road in Sagaponack, in a different friend's guest room.

Others recall Capote walking right into the middle of traffic, more or less obliviously—"absolutely out, spaced out." People rushed forth to save him when once he nearly collided with a bus.

A matter of months before he died, Alan Schwartz, Capote's attorney and close friend, received a call from a physician at Southampton hospital. Apparently Capote's brain had shrunk, its actual physical size diminishing, according to CAT scan results. If he did not stop drinking and drugging, the doctor told Schwartz, "he will be dead in six months."

"I think he just decided . . . I'm going to be stoned all the time," Knowles says. "And die."

Capote told Schwartz, "Let me go. I want to go."

In the end, where Capote went was where he often did, to the home of Joanne Carson, Johnny Carson's ex-wife, a man Capote called in *Answered Prayers* a "sadist" with a "huckleberry grin." There was a pool under eucalyptus trees, always kept bathtub-warm, where Truman sat on the top step, holding forth on summer days. For ten years Carson had more or less shut the house down, kept it very private for Capote. He'd arrive, write, swim, try getting healthy. Carson was a nutritionist, with a Ph.D. in nutrition and physiology. She'd insist that he drink carrot juice, work out in the pool. There was alcohol all over the house, Carson says, but on those occasions when Capote came to stay, "he would not drink."

In Capote's protected bedroom, two large pinatas hung from the ceiling. The bedside table was littered with candy—Snickers bars, Twix bars, licorice comfits. A teddy bear sat nearby, with the words "I love you" etched on the front—a gift from Marilyn Monroe.

This was the childhood Capote was denied, Carson a much-improved version of Nina, loving, attentive, concerned, encouraging. The two even flew kites Capote assembled from kits, just as he'd done with crazy Aunt Sook many years before; one took a nose-dive and struck a Mercedes. "We've got to get out of here," Truman shouted.

When the time came, when Capote had settled in his mind on giving up, letting himself go, he booked a one-way flight to Los Angeles—no open return. "I don't know what's happening to me," he told Carson by phone. "I didn't take any drugs, I didn't have anything to drink. . . . My body is giving up on me."

Two friends drove him to the airport on a Thursday. They knew then they would never see him alive again. On the way to Carson's house, the driver from the airport got lost; Capote became hysteri-cal. That first night at Carson's, he ate scrambled eggs, cottage cheese, tomatoes. Carson's birthday was coming. Capote asked her about a gift, what she wanted for a present. "I just want you to write," she said; "if you're writing, I'm happy."

Over four hours, Capote finished what would be his final work. It's a short reminiscence, titled "Remembering Willa Cather." In it he's ten, back in childhood, in the private, powerful world of his mind, the place he always knew he belonged, the place that never failed him, never let him down or disappointed. He recalls forty or more relatives who died during the Civil War, including his great grandfather. He remembers reading their battlefield letters, final missives written in the knowledge that death's prospects loomed, each sentence quite possibly the last, forever. He decides, at ten no less, to "write an historical book based on these Confederate heroes." But "trouble interferes," as it usually did for Capote, living in that snake's nest of No's. Yet eight years later he's back at the task, in the New York Society Library, a warm, clean, "cozy haven" in wintertime.

It is here, while researching his historical book, that he runs into "the blue-eyed lady"—yet another enchantress, another fanta-sized maternal *imago*—eyes like "a prairie dawn on a clear day." Her face is wholesome and countrified, her hair black and white and "mannishly cut"—just like Holly Golightly's was, just like Grady McNeil's, just like nearly all the hairstyles of the mad, way-ward girls of the early stories, the girls Capote secretly wanted to become.

"Fist-sized snowballs" pummel the air as the blue-eyed lady tries vainly to hail a taxi. Capote volunteers to walk her home. She smiles wordlessly. Eventually they stop, at her suggestion, for a cup of tea. Capote has something else in mind. Barely eighteen and looking far younger, per usual, he orders a double martini.

He begins with his life story, an origins tale. He tells her he was born in New Orleans. He tells her, tremulously, that he's an aspiring writer. The talk then turns to books—Flaubert, Dickens, Turgenev, Wharton, Twain, Melville.

"Oh, and I love Willa Cather," Capote gushes, singling out the books *A Lost Lady* and *My Mortal Enemy*.

The blue-eyed lady pauses, deep in thought, as if deciding on a matter of critical importance. "I wrote those books," she says.

Capote is stunned. There is, he declares, "no living person I would rather have met," Garbo included, Stalin and Gandhi, too. Cather notices his excitement. Both sit speechless for a time. Capote impulsively swallows his double martini "in one gulp."

As they part, Cather does the unexpected—she invites Capote to dinner. "And please bring some of your writing," she adds. "I'd like to read it."

The story was finished in one afternoon, out near the pool, and it reached 17 handwritten pages. A little of his power remained, still alive despite the booze, the pills, the profound fatigue. Capote had just days to live, but the words came when summoned, at least for now. Cather is an interesting choice of subject. Capote habitually eviscerated other writers in print, cleaning their clocks with devilish pleasure. Not Cather, though. Never Cather, to whom he was ferociously loyal, and whom he did in fact know personally. He called her "a great artist," an "extraordinary American writer" who deserved to be read and remembered, predicting (incorrectly, as it turns out) a revival of interest in her work. At the same time, she always warned him that he was too sensitive to criticism. She questioned the thickness of his skin, advising him to toughen up. "I used to complain to [her] about what annoyed me," he said, "which gave [her] the idea that I was overly sensitive to it but, in fact, I really wasn't. [She] said it, but it wasn't true." Cather's advice would have been on Capote's mind. The storm from *Answered Prayers* still rumbled and flashed. There was ample reason to wonder about his ability to absorb its repercussions. After all, he was at death's door. As usual, he fled into deactivating mode. She was mistaken, he wasn't too sensitive, his skin was thicker than most—he *could* take it.

In the story, Cather confirms the value of his writing—unlike Nina, unlike even Holly Golightly, the fictional character whom Fred's work bored. He's just 18, but she's interested, encouraging;

she wants to read it. That he respected her as much as he did makes these final written words, this last reminiscence, quickly understandable. He conjured a person who believed in him, a deeply reassuring, utterly unambivalent presence to offset and partially silence all the jet-set, society howlers. Cather was the perfect coda.

On the very last day, Carson rose before dawn. It was still dark. Something was bothering her. She discovered Capote trying to pull on his bathing suit, working hard to get the shorts over his hips. He "looked the color of paper." He said he felt "very fragile"—a strange word for him to use, according to Carson. He asked her to sit and talk, grabbing her hand "with the strongest grip I've ever felt in my life." She took his pulse; it was weak and fluttery. "I think I'm dying," Capote said. "No paramedics, no doctors. If you truly love me you will let me go."

He was tired, cold. He asked Carson to hold him. She cried, draped him in a blanket, pressed him close, told him how much she loved him, how much he had meant to her. He said, three times, in brilliant summary of his life's never-ending narrative, "Mama." Then it was finished. He went as he wanted to—in peace.

In a letter, Capote once remembered a childhood neighbor, a husky boy who spent the summer "digging a huge deep hole in his backyard." Truman asked him the purpose of his labor. "To get to China. See, the other side of this hole, that's China." The kid never got there. "And maybe I'll never finish *Answered Prayers*," Capote wrote, "but I keep on digging!"

In his last minutes, Capote told Carson: "No more hospitals." "Just think of me," he said, "of going to China."

No "clear mechanism of death" was the Los Angeles coroner's finding. The doctors seemed puzzled, according to Clarke. Officially they declared Capote had died of "liver disease which was complicated by phlebitis and multiple drug intoxication," though tests two weeks or so prior had shown the liver to be "pre-cirrhotic." There were no symptoms, then, of serious liver disease.

Capote had no alcohol in his blood. Just as Carson claimed, in her house he tended to stay away from drink. Yet in the hours and days before he died, he had consumed large quantities of prescription medicine: Valium (about 40 milligrams), Dilantin, codeine, and Tylenol, along with a number of barbiturates, unnamed. Clarke believes Capote was killed by "a cardiac-rhythm disorder, a disruption of the normal electrical signals to the heart," hence his fluttery pulse. "There is every possibility," in Clarke's view, "that he took a fatal overdose," whether deliberate or accidental. "Given a choice between life and death," Clarke writes, "[Capote] chose death."

Suicide is always mysterious. So much depends on intention, and intention can be hard to figure, if not impossible. People can simultaneously wish and not wish to die. If they go on living, that's fine; if they don't go on living, that's fine, too. They reach a state of deep ennui, of total disinterest, all vital essence snuffed out. There is a type of death researchers call "subintentioned." It amounts to what Clarke described: refusing to make the effort necessary to go on living.

And for Capote, after all, what was there to live for? He was disgraced. Most of his friends, or putative friends, had deserted him, erased him entirely. As Schwartz recalls, his wit had turned poisonous, his imagination distorting reality "almost beyond recognition." The book that occasioned the desertions wasn't coming, and he must have guessed, if he didn't know absolutely, that it never would. Art was always Capote's solution. Writing was his power, his strength, the one thing he never questioned. That abiding gift now gone, save for intermittent flashes, Capote was solutionless. When he wasn't high, he bored himself, so he made sure to stay high. He saw through people, Knowles says; he grew more and more disillusioned. Then he said, "To hell with this." The curtain fell, and he let it, just like the woman on the phone in *Answered Prayers* watching a body drop from the roof.

6 | PREPARATIONS FOR THE SCAFFOLD OF A PERSONALITY PORTRAIT

Researchers have carved up the self in different ways. In fact, psychology's master narrative, unrolling and refining itself over the last hundred years at least, if not longer, is one of subdivision. The mind is "a very big thing," or "no thing at all," perhaps an emergent property of brain function, or entirely separate from brain function, or identical to brain function—who knows? Whatever the case, whatever "the mind" truly is, scientists have aimed to divide and conquer, in the process splitting *personality* into manageable fragments. Now academic Psychology has more than 50 sub-disciplines, each with its own sub-sub-disciplines, each speaking a different language, nurturing different nomenclatures discouraging collaboration.

But it has been this way since the turn of the twentieth century. Freud settled, after many fits and starts, on his structural model of *id, ego, superego*, frictioned by life and death. William James had his "congress of characters," the *I, Me, Social Self* and *Spiritual Self*; Erikson his "eight ages of man," each revolving around specific decisive encounters; Jung his universal archetypes and more situationally attuned complexes, all aiming for perfect unity according to the law of compensatory function. Karen Horney described three basic modes of action in the world, each a response to anxiety: "moving towards, moving away, moving against." To Skinner, "personality" was nothing special, merely a learned "repertoire of behavior" governed by contingencies of reinforcement.

For years, disagreement prevailed; each theorist had his or her divergent take. Now the story is different. Most scientists of personality see more or less eye to eye. That there are various *levels* of personality organization, at least, seems incontestable. Minimum standards exist for what is necessary when sizing any person up—not that fights do not erupt every now and then. The agreement is not perfect, approximate rather than complete, but there does appear to be more of it than ever.

Dan McAdams, for one, homes in on five essential components. At opposite ends of the genetic and environment spectrum, there is biology—hardwired, brain-structural, chemical endowments—and culture. These two bookend scenes and scripts (stories we tell about who we are); characteristic adaptations (things like motivational dynamics and conflicts, goals, strategies, beliefs, values); and dispositional traits (namely the "Big Five" of extraversion, neuroticism, agreeableness, conscientiousness, and openness). So, who we are and what we do and how we feel all tend to be functions of these assorted vectors, some more powerful than others, depending on the fragment of personality in play at the time. McAdams, in his research, focuses mostly on stories and sequences and the role they play in structuring identity; but he does not discount variables such as biology, culture, or traits, either. All are invited to the personality party.

Robert McCrae and Paul Costa spell out a similar approach, which they call a "universal personality system." Like McAdams, they include *biological bases* (present but poorly understood vis-à-vis personality, with "precise mechanisms not yet specified"); *external influences* such as cultural norms and life events in situations; *characteristic adaptations*, here defined as habits, skills, roles, or relationships that vary across the lifespan and that "reflect the enduring psychological core of the individual"; and *traits*, or in McCrae and Costa's terms, "basic endogenous tendencies." Stories, or self-schemas, or personal myths, form the *self-concept*, which is partly a function of a person's *objective biography*, any one instance of behavior such as an emotional reaction to some sort of circumstance or perception. Interactions between these components in the system are governed by what McCrae and Costa call, vaguely, "dynamic processes." So, for instance, traits bring about characteristic adaptations, but they also affect our self-concept directly, with personal myths strongly influenced by our dispositional signature.

I mention all this as a stimulus for reflecting on Capote's personality and what we have come to know about it in the course of this book. I should add, a little tangentially, that Capote did once submit to personality testing, in Berkeley, California, under the auspices of the late Frank Barron and what was then called the "Institute of Personality Assessment and Research," or IPAR. The research concerned creativity, and Capote was tested for three straight days, according to Harrison Gough, who produced a CPI (California Psychological Inventory) analysis of Truman. Needless to say, it would be quite a coup to present Capote's CPI results here. They would be enormously interesting to sift through, providing objective data to compare with my far more subjective interpretations of Capote's life and work. I made a few efforts to obtain the CPI—to no avail. The results are buried somewhere in the Bay Area; no one knows exactly how to locate them. Perhaps they will surface some day—just like the completed manuscript of *Answered Prayers*! If and when that happens, they will either broadly confirm or call into question certain conclusions reached in this book. That is an interesting feature of psychobiography, in fact, one usually over-looked entirely. New data emerge all the time—archives open up, papers get discovered—and these materials potentially comment either positively or negatively, *post hoc*, on arguments made before their appearance.

But for now, using McAdams and McCrae and Costa as guides, we need to work with what we have. And in fact, there's quite a lot to think over. Some of what follows represents a review; some a refinement and elaboration. The goal is to step back and assess, to take a long view of who Capote was fundamentally and how those aspects that made him who he was interacted dynamically in a sort of fractionally harmonious unison.

Let's begin where McAdams and McCrae and Costa begin, with biological bases. I could argue that Capote was born with a tendency towards anxiety, and present different neurochemical, neurotrans-mitter-based models of anxiety disorder; or depression, for that matter, since Capote was often depressed. I could also claim Capote was born with alcoholism—both he and his mother drank heavily; Capote even labeled himself an "alcoholic." There is a temptation, given the unusually early appearance of Capote's narrative gifts, his verbal fluency and dexterity, to say he was born an artist. Or, who knows, a homosexual. In short, I could cobble together a number of physical models of elements of Capote's experience, but I would be chasing reductionistic rainbows. I don't want to do that. I don't see the point. I agree with McCrae and Costa—precise biological mechanisms have yet to be specified. Tantalizing findings exist, but they don't get us where we want to go. Capote's biology is inacces-sible anyway. So I suggest we set biological bases aside. They can't help us. This is no major loss, since we do know quite a bit about two other personality levels in particular: life stories/personal myths, and characteristic adaptations.

As to the former, it is clear to me that the "ouch" script and the "table-turning" script were both powerful determinants of Capote's thoughts, feelings, and behavior. He feared closeness, intimacy, and the vulnerability occasioned by seeking out love, because these things, from his earliest childhood, ended in rejection or abandonment. He expected to be hurt; he unconsciously anticipated it. And more often than not, his expectations were met. People *did* reject him, they *did* abandon him. Like scripts often do, this one became self-fulfilling. As a theory of self, "ouch" worked. It therefore also became self-*confirming*, time and again.

The same can be said of "table-turning." Sometimes Capote was simply hurt, period. The "ouch" came, and he was sad, forlorn, anxious, bereft. At other times, his "table-turning" impulse was activated, and he struck back to disprove doubters or underestimators. Why did he pounce only sometimes and not at others? My sense, albeit imperfect, is this: The "ouch" script governed rejections of his attempts at love and closeness. At its root, if we circle back to its prototypical manifestation in the hotel room at age two, it arose out of attachment and availability threats. Crucially important attachment-figures disappointed him. "Table-turning," as in Busybody and the IQ test saga, had mostly to do with Capote's assertion of power in the face of contrary assumptions. It was more agency-based than communion-based. "Table-turning" was a protest; Capote's strength kicked in, his dismissed potency. *Answered Prayers* is a fine example. Café society didn't exactly figure him for a "retard," like teachers and neighbors did; but he was cast in the role of mantelpiece object, trinket, or amusement. The *mere*-ness of that was unacceptable, infuriatingly dismissive. So the Tiny Terror appeared. Capote sliced and diced with his favorite weapon, words. He made the jet set pay.

According to McCrae and Costa, scripts or personal myths are directly, dynamically altered by characteristic adaptations.[1] They (scripts) form in the way they do because habitual reactions (characteristic adaptations) make a narrative necessary. That is, we need to tell stories about the things we keep doing over and over. This realization takes us back to attachment. And very promisingly, too, because *looking closely at how attachment-related dynamics and scripts interact goes to the very essence of Capote's personality.*

It is a certainty that Capote feared abandonment and rejection. He said so again and again. It is a virtual certainty that he was insecurely attached—about the aunts who raised him, he was ambivalent; he speaks of having no real "family"; Arch and Lillie Mae paid him scant attention, at best very marginally responsive to his needs, if at all. He moved, as he said, in a cloud of fear and anxiety. As Princess Lee Radziwill explained, he was far more neurotic than most people guessed, given his *bon vivant* façade.

As we have seen, insecurity leads to two particular adult attachment-related strategies, both characteristic adaptations. Capote was a hyperactivator—constantly on alert for attention- and availability-threats, emotionally volatile and needy—but he also used deactivation—suppressing emotion and pretending to be a lot more impervious and independent than he really was. These strategies, consistently employed, consistently on display, were folded into stories. They *had* to be, because there was a need, possibly even a brain-based need, to make sense of behaviors he watched himself engage in.[2]

---

1. I see the influence as more reciprocal, with scripts or personal myths also feeding into or even producing characteristic adaptations; McCrae and Costa do not.

2. I say "possibly even a brain-based need" because, according to research by Michael Gazzaniga, the left brain's interpreter module or language center generally refuses to leave

In Capote's case, the way in which characteristic adaptations like hyperactivation and deactivation led to script-formation is fairly clear-cut. Hyperactivation implies up-regulated anxiety, emotional lability, frantic efforts to maintain bonds, and expectations of loss (among other elements). These strategies mesh perfectly with the "ouch" script; the "ouch" script enfolds the strategies in narrative. Remember: scripts are affect-driven. Their function is to organize, interpret, manage, predict, or even reverse affect. It is a simple notion, brilliant in its implications: we tell stories in order to understand why we feel the way we do.

In hyperactivating mode—Capote's most typical "setting"— emotions are intensified, threats exaggerated, vulnerability overemphasized, and bids for attention flagrant. The "ouch" script—Capote frantic, fear-filled, and throwing tantrums in the hotel room, or forlornly drinking his mother's perfume as the big black Buick rolls away[3]—codifies hyperactivation. Sets of relationship rules and expectations are elaborated. Unconsciously and automatically, it works like this: "My history tells me that when I need love I (a) feel *vulnerable,* then I (b) feel *frightened* and *anxious,* and people (c) *threaten* to leave me; then I (d) *try to make them not go,* but they (e) *abandon* me anyway." What is involved are feelings (vulnerability, fear, anxiety); perceptions (of threat); and behaviors (efforts to elicit attention, avoid abandonment). The script essentially describes the strategies and predicts outcomes in terms of emotion and behavior (of self and others). It is a set of rules for what to do and what is most likely to occur.

---

any consequential behavior unnarrated. It even produces stories under conditions of total ignorance.

3. Or, in fictional versions of the script, Holly leaving Fred or Joel going in search of a father but finding an invalid.

McCrae and Costa draw just one causal arrow, not two, between characteristic adaptations and life stories or personal myths. The former dynamically alter the latter. I think it works both ways, however. Once the script forms, it becomes a blueprint. It is a recipe for behavior. It may arise out of the behavior initially, but it is more than the behavior, it is an emergent property, irreducible. So it alters strategies, too, just as strategies alter it. The influence is reciprocal, not unidirectional.

Deactivation and "table-turning" also mesh well. Those using deactivating strategies block emotion, down-regulate any relationship threat, exaggerate their self-reliance, doubt the goodness of the world, and avoid problem-solving because it requires openness to new information. Having little practice at it, deactivators also appraise emotion poorly. They seldom know what they are feeling. They express confusion about mood states.

Capote was a deactivator. His facade was one of derring-do and damn the torpedoes; there was that "magic pill" he used to block out feeling. He said whatever he wanted and cared little about what people thought of what he said. He certainly doubted the goodness of the world, and for good cause—parents left, murderers randomly killed entire families, mothers committed suicide, and as one of his characters alarmingly concluded, "all our acts are acts of fear." Where did this fear come from? The world. The world was fearsome. Capote was also bad at sizing up or predicting emotions. When it came to *Answered Prayers*, he failed to predict the swans' reactions; he also failed to predict his own. On one hand, they could go to hell for all he cared; on the other, their blacklisting raked him, and he never recovered, he was never the same.

One complexity about "table-turning" vis-à-vis deactivation is that "table-turning" *alters* affect, while deactivation *suppresses* it. I don't see that as a contradiction, however. Here's why. Deactivators profess "I feel nothing," like Capote did with respect to *Answered*

Prayers's fallout. Emotion is inhibited or blocked. "Table-turning" sets that "nothing" on fire with aggressive assertiveness. In this case, the script is: "I form a relationship with you that's important, but (a) you doubt me and (b) underestimate me, although (c) I don't really care all that much anyway, because (d) you can't hurt me, and (e) I'm going to prove you wrong in the long run." The deactivating strategies are obvious; the "table-turning" follows in the wake of no conscious feeling at all, or else slight anxiety at the prospect of doubt and underestimation, far less than one meets with in hyperactivators.

There has been some research (not a great deal) on correlations between levels of personality organization: in other words, how different identity-related components function together to produce cognitive, emotional, or behavioral outcomes. McAdams *et al.*, for instance, examined relationships between Big Five traits and life-story characteristics. They found, among other things, that neuroticism was positively associated with an emotionally negative life-narrative tone, and openness with structurally complex life-narrative accounts. Surprisingly, extraversion was *not* associated with positive narrative tone, despite its core element of positive emotionality.

I am not aware of any experimental or quasi-experimental work on attachment style and script formation. My analysis of Capote suggests that such a line of inquiry might prove instructive, however. Psychobiography can be generative in exactly this way: the single case highlights avenues for researchers to explore. It points to elements of theory worth tinkering with or expanding. Here, potential associations between attachment and scripts make excellent sense hypothetically because both models assume that thought and behavior serve to *regulate emotion*. Scripts are affect-driven; attachment-related strategies are, too. In each case, life is largely about interpreting, managing, predicting, and controlling feelings. Feeling is the engine (or as Tomkins said, "affect is everything").

That being so, the question of relationship quality and resulting affect becomes the first step in any exploration of a life. From there, one investigates scripts as sequelae of (1) attachment security or insecurity and (2) whatever prominent, derived affect ensues. Certain trademark types of script would be expected to come out of secure attachments; others would be expected of avoidant or anxious attachments. In short, script and attachment history ought to jibe in theoretically meaningful and coherent ways. At the very least, it is an interesting empirical question.

McAdams and McCrae and Costa agree about the importance of characteristic adaptations and stories or personal myths; they also agree, though less emphatically, about the importance of traits, or what McCrae and Costa prefer to call "basic endogenous tendencies." The trait inventory sheds light on Capote as well. Let's take a look at how, and to what degree.

These days, when psychologists refer to traits, what they mean are the Big Five of *extraversion, openness, agreeableness, conscientiousness,* and *neuroticism.* There is minor debate about whether this particular set of dimensions is *enough* or *not enough* to capture individual differences in personality expression, but for now, it represents a consensus view. The dimensions are *dichotomous*: one can score high or low on standard measures of extraversion, high or low on neuroticism. They are also partly *heritable*: one can be born with a tendency towards openness or agreeableness.

Scores of studies show that the Big Five predict behavior, too. For example, those high in neuroticism are much more likely to smoke cigarettes; those high in extraversion tend to talk more and more readily when among strangers. One's dispositional thumbprint makes a difference, in other words. Once it is identified, certain educated guesses can be made about a person's predilections.

Each trait subsumes six facets, most self-explanatory. Neuroticism, for instance, includes the elements of anxiety, anger/hostility, depression, self-consciousness, impulsiveness, and vulnerability. Extraversion represents interpersonal warmth, gregariousness, assertiveness, high activity levels, excitement-seeking, and at its core, positive emotions. The term "trait" itself, then, is shorthand for sets of characteristics it refers to and stands for.

Let's plug in Capote and see what we discover. We have assessed his characteristic adaptations and scripts, but what about his basic endogenous tendencies? The most painfully obvious conclusion is this: Capote was high in neuroticism. He was anxious, vulnerable, depressed at times, angry at times, and impulsive. Purely descriptively, he was a textbook case. And because of his neuroticism, he was beset with negative emotions. He was forced, in other words, to *do something* about his anxiety, anger, and depression. Feelings were a problem. The opposite of neuroticism is emotional stability—something Capote lacked most of the time.

In longitudinal research by Stephen Soldz and George Vaillant, 163 men were followed prospectively for over 45 years; they were rated on a set of 25 personality traits at the end of their college careers, then completed a Big Five measure—the NEO-PI—around age 67. College personality profiles were later used to "predict what happened to the men in the future." It is a remarkable, informative, and relatively rare piece of research. With respect to neuroticism (N), what the researchers found was this. It was significantly *negatively* correlated with early life adjustment, late midlife adjustment, adult life-stage reached, and maturity of defenses. Those high in N in college, therefore, turned out to be maladjusted adults who relied on unhealthy defensive mechanisms for dealing with anxiety.

This last detail is worth thinking through in relation to Capote. What was his defensive style? One classically immature defense is projection—putting one's feelings in others as a way of "getting them out" of oneself. A result can be paranoia, an attitude Capote admitted to more than once. With *Answered Prayers*, Capote sensed malevolence "out there," in the swans whose friendships he had secured. But was it more in him or in them? He came to detest the rich, he said. Their values, the way they closed ranks, stiff-armed outsiders—it all repulsed him. He felt anger and hostility. Maybe *their* anger—his perception of it—or their impulse to dismiss or reject was in fact more *his*, or at least partly his. He defensively made them more ominous than they were, so when he lashed out it seemed entirely justified. They *deserved* it—because, unconsciously, he lent them his own hatred. What he actually destroyed were the feelings he had in himself.

There are other findings from Soldz and Vaillant that also make sense. Men high in N were more likely to abuse alcohol—like Capote did. High N was associated with a family history of depression—a fact applicable to Lillie Mae.

What about other dimensions? Was Capote an extravert? I don't think so. At its core, extraversion includes strongly positive emotionality—hardly frequently present in Capote. Capote was gregarious; he was excitement-seeking. On talk shows, he was a draw; he could dish with the best of them. But little of this occurred in a context of happiness. It all seemed to have more to do with insecurity than anything else. I do think Capote, like many artists, was higher than average in *openness*. Openness includes imagination and fantasy-proneness—both obviously key to Capote's art. Those high in openness are also attuned to aesthetics, and Capote was a lover of things beautiful. Beauty was a value he held dear. Cognitively, Capote's psychology fits the openness dimension nicely.

Behaviorally, I am not so sure. Openness correlates with all four elements of sensation-seeking: experience-seeking, thrill- and adventure-seeking, boredom-susceptibility, and impulse inhibition. Capote did seek experience. He was a devoted drug-user, especially in later years, but he found cocaine, for instance, too stimulating. It interfered with his work. His preference was for depressants, like alcohol. And he was not particularly thrill-seeking. He didn't pursue adventure for its own sake. He wasn't keen on continuously trying new things, pushing his comfort level, amping up the level of stimulation. He had to be calm to write. Too much excitement got in his way. People high in openness are adventurers, explorers, adrenaline-junkies. The only place Capote really sought adventure was in the private world of his imagination, the words he strung together, the subjects he took up. He wasn't the skydiving type.

As for agreeableness and conscientiousness, neither dimension captures Capote uniquely. On balance, he was more disagreeable than agreeable. He took nasty pleasure in dismissing other writers. His pose was to care little about whom he offended. He even rubbed a few KBI agents the wrong way while researching *In Cold Blood*. And up to his last years, when he started breaking down on so many levels, Capote was marginally conscientious. He was fierce about his art. His work habits were legendary. He had a strong sense of duty and discipline. There was that whip, and he utilized it when necessary. He held himself to the highest of standards. But there were also times when he didn't come through, when he failed to "walk the talk." For instance, there was no *Answered Prayers*, despite what he claimed in interviews and on talk shows.

Just as McAdams *et al.* investigated associations between the levels of stories and traits, Eric Noftle and Phillip Shaver examined associations between attachment style (a characteristic adaptation) and traits. What they found provides support for some of the descriptive assessments ventured above. As I have said already, one thing we almost surely know about Capote is that he was anxiously attached. He said as much, and so did his close friends and lovers. So attachment anxiety makes for a solid starting point. And in keeping with my speculations about Capote's neuroticism, Noftle and Shaver found strong correlations between anxious attachment styles and all six facets of N: depression, anxiety, and vulnerability in particular. They also found a negative correlation between anxious attachment and positive emotion (a facet of extraversion). This all makes good sense, and it fits Capote perfectly. One minor misfit is this: attachment anxiety correlated *negatively* with all six facets of conscientiousness, self-discipline in particular. For most of his life, Capote was disciplined. His commitment rarely wavered. He was a serious, productive artist. Here, then, the Tiny Terror was a tiny bit anomalous. He was *conscientiously neurotic*—not markedly so, but to a degree that would have to be termed above-average. The impulsivity of Capote's neuroticism was held in check, fractionally, by his sense of duty to his work.

The blurry picture is coming into a bit more focus, but one level remains: *culture*. It is important, too. *In Cold Blood* made Capote a rich man. He was a jet-set honorary member; he was in café society. His dreams, in other words, were realized—the same dreams nurtured lovingly (and neurotically) by Lillie Mae. But Capote was not *born* that way. He was rooted in Monroeville. He came from dirt. He wasn't poor, he never lived like a sharecropper, but to the end he maintained, sometimes even insisted on, a "white trash" status. Yachts, cocktail parties, salons, and sitting rooms notwithstanding, Capote was an outsider. He was rich, but he wasn't *of* the rich. He got into the club, but he didn't *belong*. For a writer, it was almost the perfect situation. Artists are supreme outsiders. They find their way into various worlds, various milieus, then take from them what they need to produce the work they have in mind. They come and go. They don't loiter. They have no commitments or responsibilities. They lift shamelessly, answering to nothing but the work, the product. *Answered Prayers* was a declaration of his outsider status. It announced it like a roundhouse right.

But there was more. Capote had a lot of P.B. Jones in him (or vice versa). Ever the opportunist, user, and manipulator, Jones symbolizes a sociopathic artist orientation, the one Capote embodied with *Answered Prayers*. And I suspect some of this had to do with class. In effect, poor white trash showed up the jet set, toyed with it, exposed it, put it in its place, reduced it to baser realities. Jones is a little bit Perry Smith too, as is Capote. In fact, one of the things that drew Capote to Smith was class affinity. They came from the same place. They lived similar lives. They dreamed similar dreams. So Capote *qua* Smith *qua* Jones plays with power. The rich are just as trashy as the trash, maybe even trashier. They are certainly less charming, less likable, less honest. They don't survive the Southern infiltration, in other words. But they do bite back, and Capote was made to pay. Good art always exacts this kind of price. No one emerges unscathed. Capote knew that. He was fighting his own private Civil War.

With the variables now lined up, let's hazard a little dynamic arithmetic. Every chaotic bit of behavior is actually an emergent function of traits, characteristic adaptations, stories, and culture, at the very least. Take, for instance, "La Cote Basque, 1965," *Answered Prayers's* most notorious excerpt, the one that threw Capote into the hottest of hot water. Why did Capote write and publish it? Why did he bite the hands that fed him; fry the fancy fish?

First, there was his neuroticism (N), Capote's major default setting. His atmosphere was negative emotion. More often than not, he felt vulnerable, anxious, angry, and hostile; he was also impulsive, not the best moderator. It is possible, too, that Capote's hostility towards the rich was projected—N being correlated with immature defenses. So he saw his anger mirrored back. He made the jet set more fearsome than they were objectively. He upped the threat level. And when the threat level was upped, he always felt a need to respond, sometimes preemptively.

There was a slight role for openness (O), too. Partly because he was moderately high O, Capote thought creatively; he was drawn to art, interested in expressing himself imaginatively. If the rich became problematic emotionally, partly due to inborn N, one way to explore that fact was through writing about it.

Then there was his agreeableness (A). Capote was slightly low A. He let the negativity fly. He never minded wounding, telling it like it is. He was not a peacekeeper, but a shit-stirrer, as some called him. High A writers would never contemplate writing *Answered Prayers*. Being low A, Capote felt less compunction. His goal was to offend.

Now, one might stop right here, in effect laying all Capote's motives at the "traits" door. Some do just this. Some find traits sufficient for effective understanding. I don't. To me, traits are essential first considerations, but insufficient singly or in amalgamation. More has to happen.

As we have seen, traits and attachment interact. Those high in attachment anxiety tend also to be high N. Capote is a case in point, a perfect illustration. Those who are high N are not typically securely attached. High N theoretically sets a person up for attachment insecurity because relationships get transacted anxiously and self-consciously, in a context of heightened vulnerability. What this means is that even if Capote had had the most attentive and responsive of parents, he still would have felt unjustified amounts of insecurity. But Capote had the opposite; his parents rejected and abandoned him. Insult (rejection) was added to native injury (N). In other words, Capote was *made* to feel insecure about love, and he was *born* N, to boot. He lived in a state of anxiety squared. Threat was everywhere, and he increased its intensity via projection.

Does attachment anxiety cause N or does N cause attachment anxiety? Who can say for sure? Answers depend, as always, on theory allegiances. If N is indeed partly heritable, then it is there, so to speak, when we begin relating to others. But if these others are unavailable and unresponsive, then that only inflames N, intensifies it. Linear causality is never the best explanatory avenue to pursue in psychobiography. One needs to think, instead, of reciprocal interactions, dynamisms. Reality is mixed and messy, more Pollock than Pointillism.

Capote's neurotic miasma of attachment anxiety forced him to evolve the strategies we have examined closely—hyperactivation and deactivation. Because the rich were "disloyal," as he put it, and because he never believed in their love, he abandoned them prophylactically. Neurotically, he hurt himself to avoid getting hurt, but then, apropos of deactivation, he denied the hurt, mocked it, dismissed it: "You are likely to hurt me so I'll hurt you first and it won't (will) hurt me to do so."

Capote's emerging key scenes and scripts placed N and attachment anxiety into story packages. His conflicts were narrated; they assumed form. He expected pain, and he got it. It was a *fait accompli*, his biography told him. But he turned the tables, too; he tossed his handmade bomb, it blew him up, and the damage was collateral. I say this with some reluctance, but Capote was a destroyer. If he failed to get what he needed, the arsonist in him came out. "La Cote Basque, 1965" was self-immolation, leaving no one unsinged.

Culture is the final vector. It operates at the broadest level, as a kind of master narrative. "La Cote Basque, 1965" was white-trash triumph. The interloper flexed his outsider muscles, making a mockery of privilege and prestige. This was class warfare. Everyone died.

Any instance of Capote's behavior can be looked at in this way, as emergent function. His reaction to his mother's suicide, Perry's death, Capote's conflict surrounding homosexuality, the desire to write *In Cold Blood*, the invention of a character like Holly Golightly—all involve, to different degrees, and in different combinations and strengths, traits, characteristic adaptations, scripts, and culture. Each decision, each behavior, each feeling is a little *Gestalt*, a complex whole made up of interrelated dynamic parts. This is important to keep in mind. The impulse is to single out part-processes, privilege one vector over others or dismiss certain vectors entirely. That is ill-advised. The best principle is over-determination. The self is a choir, not a soloist. Harmony may not emerge, but each singer contributes her part.

And what about Capote's "consistent inconsistency," his sense, of a sort many people have—for instance the writer Patricia Highsmith, a friend of Capote's—that he was not just one, but a *handful* of persons, more plurality than unity? Depending on the trait, adaptation, and script conglomeration active in any one moment of thought, feeling, and behavior, Capote would have seemed like a different person, to himself and others. When his neuroticism was especially active, when he was in hyperactivation mode, when the "ouch" script kicked into gear, he was anxious, vulnerable, full of negative emotion, expecting to be hurt and injured. When he was disagreeable, in deactivation mode, with the "table-turning" script turned on, he was nasty, corrosive, unfeeling, and bent on exacting revenge, making people pay for their dismissals of him. These were Capote's most prominent dual personalities: neurotic Capote, fear-filled and injury-prone; and Capote the disagreeable destroyer, emotionally bulletproof. They fluctuated, and they lent his life a quality of dividedness. Either the world itself was a threat, or Capote was a threat to the world. Whatever the case, something nasty was going on. It is a sense, of foreboding mainly, that Capote put in the heads of his characters, especially the haunted men of the early stories, who keep getting victimized and keep reaching the same conclusions. Fear was inescapable.

Capote died a sad, lonely death. In some ways he scripted it. He never expected to be loved; he expected to be dismissed, and he was in the end. He made it happen. The rule applied. With *Other Voices*, Capote claimed to have left the boy behind. But really, Joel Knox was always there. Capote traveled far and wide to find love in the ways he knew how, some actually destructive. But if it came, it didn't stay. It died, like Perry. Killed itself, like Lillie Mae. Wound up mute and brain-damaged, like father-figure Mr. Samson. Or disappeared into Africa, like Holly Golightly. Even the swans flew off, to the sound of Capote's buckshot.

It sure was some sound, though. And we are all still hearing it.

NOTES ON SOURCES

A decision was made not to clog the text with referencing or more than occasional footnotes. In what follows I therefore want to provide information on *some* of the more important sources for each chapter, mainly those pertaining to Capote's life or what he said about it. In contrast, when I cite a work *by* Capote—such as *Other Voices, Other Rooms*—the source is obvious.

The following books were relied on more than any others in piecing together the facts of Capote's life. For each chapter, I refer to these sources (listed below) through the use of the author's initials (GC for Gerald Clarke, and so on; for Capote's letters, I use the initials TC). Other essential references I provide more fully in the chapter-by-chapter breakdown that follows this list.

GC: Gerald Clarke, *Capote: A Biography* (New York: Simon & Schuster, 1988).

TC: Gerald Clarke (ed.), *Too Brief a Treat: The Letters of Truman Capote* (New York: Vintage, 2004).

LG: Lawrence Grobel, *Conversations with Capote* (New York: NAL Books, 1985).

MTI: M. Thomas Inge (ed.), *Truman Capote Conversations* (Jackson, Miss.: University Press of Mississippi, 1987).

GP: George Plimpton, *Truman Capote: In Which Various Friends, Enemies, Acquaintances, and Detractors Recall His Turbulent Career* (New York: Doubleday, 1997).

INTRODUCTION: A SHORT PSYCHOBIOGRAPHY PRIMER

The best introductions to psychobiography, for those interested in reading more about the discipline, are my own *Handbook of Psychobiography*

(New York: Oxford University Press, 2005) and Alan Elms's *Uncovering Lives: The Uneasy Alliance of Biography and Psychology* (New York: Oxford University Press, 1993). Both include psychobiographical essays, as well as sections on effective methodological practices. William Runyan's *Life Histories and Psychobiography* (New York: Oxford University Press, 1984), the first book of its kind, presents wide-ranging ideas on the place of psychobiography within psychology, on epistemology, and on controversies within and surrounding the field. These three books together are indispensable for those wanting more information about the field, or thinking about embarking on a psychobiography of their own.

Other good sources for information on psychobiography include Irving Alexander's *Personology: Method and Content in Personality Assessment and Psychobiography* (Durham, N.C.: Duke University Press, 1990) and Daniel Ogilvie's *Fantasies of Flight* (New York: Oxford University Press, 2003).

For a pointed discussion of what psychobiography is, why it is important and valuable, the characteristics of good and of bad psychobiography, and the current state of the field, see my chapter "Introducing Psychobiography" (pp. 3–18) in *Handbook of Psychobiography*.

A famous paper by William Runyan explores the nature of psychobiographical explanations: "How to Critically Evaluate Alternative Explanations of Life Events: The Case of Van Gogh's Ear" (pp. 96–103) in *Handbook of Psychobiography*.

I also maintain—fitfully—an online resource. The web address is http://williamtoddschultz.wordpress.com

There aren't too many full-length psychobiographies. The sharpest, in my view, is Dan McAdams's own *Inner Lives* title, the book preceding this one in the series: *George W. Bush and the Redemptive Dream: A Psychological Portrait* (New York: Oxford University Press, 2010). I also enjoyed reading John Gartner's *In Search of Bill Clinton: A Psychological Biography* (New York: St. Martin's Press, 2008). It is a bit too diagnostic for my taste, but still occasionally insightful, especially on the relationship between Clinton and his flamboyant mother.

CHAPTER 1: CONSISTENTLY INCONSISTENT CONSISTENCY

For the hotel room lock-in story, see GC, p. 14; GP, p. 26; and LG, p. 48.

For more on Busybody, see MTI, p. 21; and LG, p. 53.

Eugene Walter's remarks on Busybody come from GP, pp. 15–16.

CHAPTER 2: A SNAKE'S NEST OF NO'S

Capote's immensely colorful childhood history is captured through recollections by intimates in GP, pp. 3–36. A lot of the information on Monroeville and Capote's aunts comes from these pages.

A broader view of Capote's early life is contained in GC, pp. 3–64.

Lawrence Grobel interviews Capote about his growing up in LG, pp. 45–58.

Many other interviews touch on Capote's childhood. For some of those, see MTI.

The IQ test tale comes from LG, p. 52; MTI, p. 117; and MTI, p. 23.

The ideal source for details on the nuances of script theory is Silvan Tomkins's wide-ranging article "Script Theory," from 1987, published in *The Emergence of Personality* (Aronoff, Rabin, & Zucker [eds.], New York: Springer Press). What some consider a more digestible overview is Rae Carlson's essay "Exemplary Lives: The Use of Psychobiography for Theory Development," in *Journal of Personality*, 1988, vol. 56.

I lay out the various elements of the prototypical-scene concept in a chapter from *Handbook of Psychobiography* titled, "How to Strike Psychological Paydirt in Biographical Data," pp. 42–63. There the lives of Kathryn Harrison, Sylvia Plath, Diane Arbus, Jack Kerouac, and even Truman Capote are mined for prototypical-scene features. An earlier, less fleshed-out chapter on prototypical scenes can be found in McAdams's, Josselson's, and Lieblich's *Turns in the Road: Narrative Studies of Lives in Transition* (Washington, D.C.: APA Press, 2001). It's called "The Prototypical Scene: A Method for Generating Psychobiographical Hypotheses." In my view one of the very best applications of the prototypical-scene hypotheses to an individual life is Nicole Barenbaum's chapter in *Handbook of Psychobiography* titled, "Four, Two, or One? Gordon Allport and the Unique Personality," pp. 223–239. Still another poignant application of prototypical phenomena is Daniel Ogilvie's chapter on James Barrie, "Margaret's Smile." It is also in *Handbook of Psychobiography*, pp. 175–187.

The history of attachment research is a very long one, stretching over many decades. For Capote, the work I rely on most is by Phillip Shaver and Mario Mikulincer. For an excellent overview of the concepts of hyperactivating and deactivating strategies, see *Handbook of Attachment (second ed.): Theory, Research, and Clinical Applications* (Jude Cassidy & Phillip Shaver [eds.], Guilford Press, 2008). The Mikulincer/Shaver chapter is titled "Adult Attachment and Emotion Regulation," pp. 503–531. Shaver's website address is http:// psychology.ucdavis.edu/faculty/Shaver/. A number of articles can be downloaded from there.

See also, in the same book, Jude Cassidy's "The Nature of a Child's Ties" (pp. 3–22) and Roger Kobak's and Stephanie Madsen's "Disruptions in Attachment Bonds: Implications for Theory, Research, and Clinical Intervention" (pp. 23–47).

CHAPTER 3: LEAVING THE BOY BEHIND?

Capote's points about style and personality can be found in MTI, p. 29.

What Capote says about the autobiographical component of *Other Voices, Other Rooms*, how its writing was an exorcism, is laid out in the book's preface, pp. ix–x.

Capote's allusion to *Other Voices*'s "secret," its meaning lying in the last few pages, is in TC, pp. 401–402.

The best source for information about Newton Arvin—his relationship with Truman and his eventual scandalous fall—is GC, pp. 104–130. Capote's reaction to Arvin's arrest is recorded in TC, pp. 291–293. There, in a footnote, Clarke provides details about what Arvin was accused of doing and how the case was resolved.

Capote's comments on the film *Breakfast at Tiffany's* are from MTI, p. 160 and p. 317—it is on page 317 that he discusses his preference for Monroe in the title role. There is more on this subject, including what Capote says about Jodie Foster, in LG, pp. 157–158.

Michener's theory about who Holly really was is from LG, p. 6. Doris Lilly's contention that *she* was Holly is from GP, p. 164. Still more on sources of inspiration for Holly are found in GC, pp. 314–315.

Capote's comments concerning Holly as an American geisha are from MTI, pp. 141–142.

Alan Schwartz provides the background on how *Summer Crossing* came to be discovered as well as the decision about whether or not to publish, in the novel's Afterword, pp. 132–138.

Capote's remark about tearing *Summer Crossing* up is in TC, pp. 216. His earlier comments about its progress are also in TC, p. 73 and p. 99.

CHAPTER 4: THE MIND OF A MURDERER

No subject has received more attention than Capote's *In Cold Blood*, the focus of two recent films, *Capote* and *Notorious*, not to mention the older, eponymous film starring Robert Blake as Perry Smith.

For a vivid picture of the struggles of the writing process itself, the letters are an excellent resource. See TC, pp. 273–426.

Capote is interviewed about the book in LG, pp. 109–128.

Another terrific interview is George Plimpton's "The Story Behind a Nonfiction Novel," in MTI, pp. 47–68. Also, MTI, pp. 118–138.

Plimpton's oral biography is an indispensable source. See in particular GP, pp. 166–226.

Gerald Clarke's section on *In Cold Blood* begins on page 318 and extends to page 365.

The article by J.J. Maloney is titled "In Cold Blood: A Dishonest Book." It can be accessed online at http://www.crimemagazine.com.

For Perry's dream of the yellow parrot, see *In Cold Blood*, pp. 92–93. For the short autobiographies the killers composed, see *In Cold Blood* again, pp. 273–279.

Nye's theory of Capote and Smith being lovers is in GP, pp. 188–189.

CHAPTER 5: FRYING FANCY FISH

The best broad overviews of *Answered Prayers* are these: LG, pp. 199–210; GP, pp. 437–451 and pp. 338–355; and GC, pp. 404–473.

Norman Mailer's reaction to *In Cold Blood* is from GP, pp. 214–215.

The Kenneth Tynan review is described by Kathleen Tynan in GP, pp. 216–217. See also GC, pp. 364–365.

Capote's drug–addled breakdown on the Stanley Siegel show, its "lunatic brilliance," is from GC, pp. 519–520. It is also recounted in MTI, p. 340, and LG, p. 211.

Capote describes the creative crisis ensuing in the wake of *In Cold Blood* in the preface to his book *Music for Chameleons* (New York: Random House, 1975).

Slim Keith's story of Capote as mantelpiece bibelot is from GP, p. 288.

Capote's comment about *Answered Prayers* being "the only true thing I know" is in MTI, p. 333. The remark about not wanting to finish the book, and finishing being tantamount to taking it out in the yard and shooting it in the head, is from MTI, p. 302. In fact, much of this interview with Jann Wenner focuses on *Answered Prayers*. The pages to consult are 301–307.

Theories about the existence or nonexistence of *Answered Prayers* are assembled in GP, pp. 437–451. Joseph Fox also reviews a number of these theories in *Answered Prayers*'s "Editor's Note," pp. xi–xxii.

The facts about the Ann Woodward case are from GC, pp. 463–467.

The "I love you" and "No, you don't" exchange with Slim Keith is in GP, p. 156.

Kate Harrington's description of Capote's "colossal depression" is contained in GP, p. 355.

Capote's final weeks are summarized in GP, pp. 408–435.

Gerald Clarke's examination of Capote's death, his deliberate or accidental overdose, is in GC, pp. 546–547.

CHAPTER 6: PREPARATIONS FOR THE SCAFFOLD OF A PERSONALITY PORTRAIT

The ideal source for McAdams's thoughts on personality's constituent elements is a 2006 article he co–wrote with Jennifer Pals titled, "A New Big Five: Fundamental Principles for an Integrative Science of Personality" (*American Psychologist*, vol. 61, pp. 204–217). He envisions how these principles might help inform psychobiography in the similarly themed chapter, "What Psychobiographers Might Learn from Personality Psychology," in *Handbook of Psychobiography*, pp. 64–83.

My source for what I say about five-factor theory is Robert McCrae and Paul Costa's chapter, "The Five Factor Theory of Personality" from *Handbook of Personality: Theory and Research*, edited by Oliver John, Richard Robins, and Lawrence Pervin, published by the Guilford Press (2008), pp. 159–181.

Two somewhat old but still enormously informative chapters on extraversion and openness, respectively, are these: "Extraversion and Its Positive Emotional Core," by David Watson and Lee Anna Clark; and "Conceptions and Correlates of Openness to Experience," by Robert McCrae and Paul Costa. Both chapters can be found in *Handbook of Personality Psychology* (New York: Academic Press, 1997), Robert Hogan, John Johnson, and Stephen Briggs, editors.

The seminal article on correlations between openness and depression is Miriam Wolfenstein and Timothy Trull's "Depression and Openness to Experience," *Journal of Personality Assessment* (1997), vol. 69, pp. 614–632.

"Traits and Stories: Links Between Dispositional and Narrative Features of Personality" is the source for details about correlations between the story and the trait levels. The article was written by Dan McAdams, Nana Akua Anyidoho, Chelsea Brown, Ti Yang Huang, Bonnie Kaplan, and Mary Anne Machado, and published in *Journal of Personality* (2004), vol. 72, pp. 761–784.

For more on the longitudinal study of traits and the life course, see Stephen Soldz and George Vaillant, "The Big Five Personality Traits and the Life Course: A 45-Year Longitudinal Study" in *Journal of Research in Personality* (1999), vol. 33, pp. 208–232.

Associations between attachment style and the Big Five traits are explored in "Attachment Dimensions and the Big Five Personality Traits: Associations and Comparative Ability to Predict Relationship Quality," by Erik Noftle and Phillip Shaver, *Journal of Research in Personality* (2006), vol. 40, pp. 179–208.

INDEX